"*The Journey Home* is devotional, part biogra it beautifully unpacks the simple-yet-profound lessons to be learned when we trace God's good purposes in our suffering. Christ-centered and full of gritty faith, this book offers real hope and comfort to those who have been touched by pain and loss in this life. It deeply ministered to my own soul, and I highly recommend it."

– Scott Anderson, Executive Director

Desiring God Ministries

"We give our patients hope, but you give me hope. I love seeing your smile each time you come for your clinic visit. It brightens my day. The world is a better place because you have been here."

– Dr. Katy Peters,

Duke University Brain Tumor Center

The Holy Bible, King James Version

The Holy Bible, New King James Version (NKJV) Copyright © 1982 by Thomas Nelson, Inc. Used by permission.

New Century Version®. (NCV) Copyright © 1987, 1988, 1991 by Word Publishing, a division of Thomas Nelson, Inc. All rights reserved. Used by permission.

The Holman Christian Standard Bible™ (HCSB) Copyright © 1999, 2000, 2001 by Holman Bible Publishers. Used by permission.

The Holy Bible, New International Version®. (NIV) Copyright © 1973, 1978, 1984 International Bible Society. Used by permission of Zondervan. All rights reserved.

The Holy Bible. New Living Translation (NLT) copyright © 1996 Tyndale Charitable Trust. Used by permission of Tyndale House Publishers.

The New American Standard Bible®, (NASB) Copyright © 1960, 1962, 1963, 1968, 1971, 1972, 1973, 1975, 1977, 1995 by The Lockman Foundation. Used by permission.

The Holy Bible, English Standard Version (ESV) is adapted from the Revised Standard Version of the Bible, copyright Division of Christian Education of the National Council of the Churches of Christ in the U.S.A. All rights reserved.

Scripture taken from The Message. (MSG) Copyright © 1993, 1994, 1995, 1996, 2000, 2001, 2002. Used by permission of NavPress Publishing Group.

Cover Design by Kim Russell / Wahoo Designs
Page Layout by Bart Dawson

ISBN 978-0-9892629-0-3

Printed in the United States of America

1 2 3 4 5—CHG—17 16 15 14 13

Dr. Gene Baillie

The JOURNEY HOME

Walking Through and Rising Above
Times of Hardship and Pain

Table of Contents

Acknowledgements

I want to thank and praise God for giving me the ability to write the important truths in this book. He created the universe and all that is in it, is light for the path we walk, has adopted us into His family for eternity, and has given us His Word with promises and provision for our daily needs. We have been the recipient of God's direction and grace throughout our journey, following His leading, and seeing Him guide our every step—while holding our hands, especially in the midst of trials. May He receive the glory and honor for what He has begun, is doing, and will continue to do in and through our lives, and to each who reads this book!

Dr. Baillie offers a special thanks to Criswell Freeman, who helped immensely in writing and organizing this book. Gene observed, "Criswell helped me make sense of 50 years of marriage to the wife of my life. He helped us take just what was needed from our lives to point people to Jesus as the answer to their every need, especially during the toughest trials of life."

Dr. Baillie also wishes to thank to Dr. Dale Treash, for giving so much of his time during the writing and editing process. Dale was never afraid to ask tough questions concerning the content and the goals of *The Journey Home*. His help and encouragement were invaluable in the completion of this book, as was his solid scriptural advice concerning its contents.

A Message to Readers

———⟡———

I n January 2011, Gini, my wife of 49 years, began teaching a *Trusting God* Bible study, based on a book written by Jerry Bridges. Three months later, on Monday, April 18, 2011, she was diagnosed with brain cancer. Since then, after undergoing a complex surgery and a string of follow-up treatments, she has been an example of courage and faith. But, her journey through this terrible illness has been difficult. Little did we all know how important "trusting God" would become!

In the early stages of Gini's treatment, we focused not only on healing—which at the time seemed a distant hope at best—but also on death: what it would be like, how it would feel, when it might happen. On one occasion, when I asked Gini if she had any thoughts for others who were going through a trial or facing death (as she was the one going through it, not me), she replied, "You're going through this, too!" At that moment, I realized that my wife had spoken a profound truth: because she and I *are* one, I was enduring the trial right along with her. I, too, was facing death—both hers *and* mine.

This book contains the lessons that Gini and I have learned during our own journey through sickness and grief and pain and worry. What we've learned—or perhaps I should say "relearned," because we've had to learn these things time and again—is that God is good, that His love is everlasting, and that He has a perfect plan for each of us.

I've chosen to divide this text into 30 chapters, each of which contains an important milestone that we've passed on our journey homeward. You may find it helpful to use these messages as a daily, one-month devotional text. Or you may, instead, turn first to the chapters that apply to your own journey through (and beyond) tough times. Either way, please know that Gini and I pray that our experiences will point you to Jesus for your every need, and, in some small way, serve to light your path and strengthen your faith.

On that significant day when Gini reminded me that she and I were "in this thing together," I asked her for a single piece of advice, a kernel of wisdom that she could share with me and with the world. Without hesitation, she answered, "Just rest in the Lord." Those five words are the foundation of this text.

The Bible promises "Thou will keep him in perfect peace, whose mind is stayed on Thee." And, it promises that "the peace of God that surpasses all understanding will guard your hearts and minds in Christ Jesus." What a joy it is to realize that we can rest and trust in a Sovereign God who controls every detail of our lives.

Gini and I, like you, are on the journey of a "lifetime," an all-too-brief sojourn between the cradle and the grave. And what a glorious journey it has been for us. Despite our recent challenges, Gini and I know that we have been richly blessed by a loving God and a loving family. We believe that God's purpose in blessing us is that we might be a blessing to others.

Although we don't fully understand our Father's plans, we do know where He is leading. He is leading us beyond the inevitable challenges of everyday life. He is leading us beyond the physical pain of sickness and beyond the emotional pain of loss. He is leading us to Himself and to His Son. He is leading us home.

He invites us to trust, follow, and rest in Him. When we do, we know that whatever happens in this world, we are secure today, tomorrow, and throughout all eternity.

Testimony of
Virginia (Gini) Wagner Baillie

Five years before she was diagnosed with brain cancer,
Gini wrote this testimony as a prologue to her will.
You will see Gini met Jesus and then Jesus
walked with and guided her the rest of her life.

I was born and raised on a farm in eastern Nebraska. My parents, one brother, and I went to a Lutheran church and Sunday school almost every week in my home town of 800. When I was about 12 years old, I attended Catechism classes two hours each Saturday for two years, and at the end of that time I was "confirmed." I went to a one-room country school, worked hard on the farm, and, from the world's perspective, I was not rebellious. But from God's perspective, though very "religious," I was rotten to the core of my being. Then, in 1978, God, in grace, plucked me as a brand from the fire at age 34. As part of my life experiences, I claim, along with Timothy, that from childhood I knew the sacred writings which God used to give me the wisdom that leads to salvation through faith in Christ Jesus. The verse is found in 2 Timothy 3:15.

As to the particulars of my salvation experience, God called Gene and me to do a one-month medical mission trip to Korea, Japan, and Taiwan in the fall of 1978. Shortly before we left for the trip, my dad, at age 63, had a heart attack and I faced the mortality of those I love, as well as my own inevitable death. My mother was very anxious about us leaving the country and leaving behind our three daughters, who were 8, 12, and 14. She felt we should just donate the money that the trip would cost to the mission field. But God wanted us to experience what total dependence upon Him looked like.

When our airplane landed in Seoul, due to a communication break-down, no one was at the airport to meet us. We were unable to make telephone contact with our new missionary friends until nearly 10 p.m., which, the police at the airport informed us, was Seoul's curfew. We took a taxi to The Airport Hotel and found our room to be dirty and dingy. When we went downstairs for dinner (a bottled Coke with a straw and a piece of toast because I was afraid of getting T.B.), we asked the English-speaking manager why the bottom of the door to our hotel room was two to three inches off the floor. "So that if rats get into the room they won't chew up our doors in order to get out," was his reply.

I distinctly remember going back to the room and praying with Gene in earnest, "Lord, when we left America, we committed this time to You—but now we really MEAN it!"

Throughout the time in Korea, God opened our eyes to how much we, as Americans, depended upon ourselves as well as our government for provision and protection, thinking the whole time that we were depending upon God. Our Food and Drug Administration makes sure that restaurants are clean and serve proper food; our Federal Highway Department makes sure roads and bridges are safe and up to standard; and then, of course, our military...

Being so close to the DMZ, we experienced a blackout one night when we were far out in the country. Soldiers ran out of the ditch and began hitting the car and yelling in Korean. I was thankful for our Korean-speaking friend who could understand their instructions to turn off our car lights immediately.

We had the privilege of staying in the guest house of a missionary surgeon and, for the first time, witnessed that the God of Sundays is also the God of the rest of the week, as the doctor shared the gospel and prayed with, and for, every patient he ministered to. He and his wife had a relationship with Jesus Christ in a way that we had never seen. From that village, we spent a week in a leprosy colony where Korean lepers and their families lived and made their livings raising chickens, hogs, and rice. Many were terribly disfigured, and those who were the most debilitated lived in "The Happy House." My stomach churned as I looked at the outward appearance of these people who were missing facial features and limbs, and yet there was something different about them that seemed to glow.

As the week progressed, we discovered that many of the men got together daily to memorize scripture. Since most were blind and few had fingers with which they could read Braille, the only way to "read" scripture was to be read to. After years of hungering to hide God's Word in their hearts, nearly all had memorized the New Testament, and many had huge sections of the Old Testament on which they could regularly meditate.

We were told of a recent visit by government officials from the U.S. They toured the colony and met with some of the leading representatives. When asked what America could do to help the colony of Soonchun, the colony's leaders asked if they could have 24 hours to think through, talk out, and pray about this generous offer. The Americans left the colony with dollar signs and food and supplies going through their minds. The next day they met with the elders to hear their requests and stood in awe when they heard these words: "We have very little money or material possessions, so are unable to do much, but we have heard that in the United States of America there are many who do not know Jesus Christ yet. Therefore we have taken up a collection among our people to send back money to help support the mission work being done there."

And so, you see, God's Holy Spirit used testimonies in my life to bring about the fullness of the Truths of His Word that I had been taught through the years. Since that time, I have fallen more and more in love with my risen Lord and Savior, and I seek opportunities to tell what Christ has meant in my life. I am always aware that in my words and actions I may have the opportunity of being a part of God's plan for salvation in someone's life. And, for others, I may be the only Jesus they will ever see.

CHAPTER 1

Your Journey

You will show me the path of life;
in Your presence is fullness of joy;
at Your right hand are pleasures forevermore.
Psalm 16:11 NKJV

A LESSON FOR THE JOURNEY

Your life is a journey, and you're heading for home.

L ife here on earth is a journey that includes a perfectly predictable destination: death. But, despite the fact that death is an ever-present reality in our lives, most of us don't focus on it. Instead, we direct our attention to other things. We have jobs to do, places to go, and people to see. So, when the alarm goes off, we jump out of bed and begin the drill, often rushing from place to place, struggling with—and sometimes thinking we have risen above—the challenges of everyday living. But we don't spend much time contemplating the end of life.

For most of us, death seems a distant point on the far horizon, an event that will surely happen "some day" (hopefully not soon), a stark truth we will deal with "later." Although Gini and I did have conversations about the end of life, and despite the fact that we both understood the importance of making our lives count for something, we were not fully prepared for the stark reality of death that confronted us when she was diagnosed with an aggressive form of brain cancer. At the moment of her diagnosis, everything changed. Death became very real to us—and in a strangely beautiful way, the reality of death became a blessing. Let me explain.

If either Gini or I had passed away suddenly, or after a brief illness, we might never have experienced the shock of a deadly diagnosis, and we certainly would never have endured the trials associated with lengthy treatments. But

God had other plans: He allowed us to go through these trials for a reason.

Because we know that God's hand touches all things—because we know that He is in charge of every detail of our lives—we now believe, more than ever, that the Lord graciously allowed us to live long enough to think more rationally about the end of our journey on this earth. He has given us time, not only to contemplate the inevitability of death, but also to write frankly about the purpose of the journey that precedes it.

Gini and I know that we are on our journey home. We are traveling through and beyond the hardships of this world, to our real home, a place that is so different from the world we inhabit today that we can scarcely imagine it. And, we find peace in the knowledge that our *real* journey is only beginning.

While we cannot begin to relate all that is in our hearts and minds, we can tell of the Lord working in our own lives and in the lives of others. Time and again, we have seen Him at work in the midst of what some might describe as the darkest hour. And of this you can be sure: God is at work in your life, too.

Wherever you find yourself, whether your journey has led to the highest mountaintop or into the darkest valley, God is your constant companion, gently guiding you, sometimes correcting your course, but always leading you homeward, toward Himself and His Son.

The next time you encounter tough times—and you will—you'll have several choices to make. You can either cast God aside or hold fast to His promises. You can either give in to self-pity, or you can thank the Lord for His blessings. You can either curse your "bad luck," or you can search for the purpose that God has in store for you. These are the kinds of choices that Gini and I have faced on our own journey home. We've chosen to trust God completely and without reservation. Because of that choice, we continue to recognize His blessings.

After her diagnosis, I asked Gini what advice she would give someone facing death, and she immediately answered, "Rest and trust in the Lord." Then, she quoted Philippians 4:8: "And the peace of God that transcends understanding, will guard your hearts and minds in Christ Jesus."

I can offer no better advice for our own journey *or* for yours.

LIGHT FOR OUR PATH FROM GOD'S WORD

By faith Abraham obeyed when he was called to go out to a place that he was to receive as an inheritance. And he went out, not knowing where he was going. By faith he went to live in the land of promise, as in a foreign land, living in tents with Isaac and Jacob, heirs with him of the same promise. For he was looking forward to the city that has foundations, whose designer and builder is God.

Hebrews 11:8-10 ESV

Who is there who speaks and it happens, unless the Lord has ordained it?

Lamentations 3:37 HCSB

A man's steps are from the Lord; how then can man understand his way?

Proverbs 20:24 ESV

For My thoughts are not your thoughts, nor are your ways My ways, says the LORD. "For as the heavens are higher than the earth, so are My ways higher than your ways, and My thoughts than your thoughts."

Isaiah 55:8-9 NKJV

I came that they may have life, and have it abundantly.

John 10:10 NASB

MORE IMPORTANT IDEAS ABOUT
YOUR JOURNEY

We aren't just thrown on this earth like dice tossed across a table. We are lovingly placed here for a purpose.

Charles Swindoll

In the great orchestra we call life, you have an instrument and a song, and you owe it to God to play them both sublimely.

Max Lucado

We die daily. Happy are those who daily come to life as well.

George MacDonald

The measure of a life, after all, is not its duration but its donation.

Corrie ten Boom

Life is a glorious opportunity.

Billy Graham

Each of us may be sure that if God sends us on stony paths He will provide us with strong shoes, and He will not send us out on any journey for which He does not equip us well.

Alexander MacLaren

GINI'S JOURNEY

Gini's Smile

*Hear my prayer, O Lord, and give ear to my cry;
hold not your peace at my tears! For I am a sojourner
with you, a guest, like all my fathers. Look away from me,
that I may smile again, before I depart and am no more!*
Psalm 39:12-13 ESV

The 39th Psalm has special meaning for Gini and for me. During her illness, my wife's beautiful smile has continued to touch the hearts of believers and non-believers alike. Despite the challenges she's faced and the hardships she's endured, Gini's joyful spirit still shines brightly and often.

Psalm 39:12-13 are difficult verses to understand, but after a careful reading of the text, I have come to the conclusion that these verses speak volumes about Gini's journey. God has answered our weeping and groaning attempts at prayer to allow Gini the time and the strength to share her smile with the world. And, the Lord has given me the opportunity to write down her thoughts, as well as my own, before we "depart."

Today, Gini's smile still captivates family, friends, and strangers. It's the very same smile that I came to love so many years ago.

On one occasion, I asked Gini if she knew that the Lord had given her time *to smile again*. And, I asked if she knew that God was using her smile as a way of witnessing to the world.

She replied, "I did not know He was using it until I got sick."

Gini and I pray that you can look beyond the immediate and see the eternal. May you find reason to smile amidst the trial that is before you. Corrie ten Boom correctly observed, "There is nothing anybody else can do that can stop God from using us. We can turn everything into a testimony." And so it is with Gini's smile.

—∾—

CHAPTER 2

God Has a Plan for Your Journey

A man's heart plans his way,
but the Lord determines his steps.

—

Proverbs 16:9 HCSB

A LESSON FOR THE JOURNEY

—∾—

Every phase of your life's journey is planned—
and completed—by God.

L ife is a short journey started, orchestrated, and finished by the Lord. God places each of us here on
this earth with His predetermined purpose for our
own particular journey. He has a plan for every aspect of
that journey, including its ending.

Philippians 1:6 promises that "He who began a good
work in us will complete it in the day of Christ Jesus."
That promise gives us comfort, especially during times of
pain and hardship. We trust that God will continue to
work in us and through us until His plans are completed.

When Gini was diagnosed with cancer, she and I
prayed that God would use our experiences to comfort
others. We trusted God's timetable, and we trusted His
plan for our lives. Because of that trust, our journey, while
not easy, has been blessed. We have experienced countless moments of joy, many opportunities to minister, and
special times with family and friends. We've continued to
read God's Word and share its message. And, we've exchanged encouraging words, smiles, hugs, and prayers with
more people than we can count. In short, we know that
God's plan for us is to trust, follow, and experience Him
fully—every day.

Proverbs 16:9 is my life verse, a constant reminder of
God's sovereign control over every detail, including His
directing every step I take. Yet He allows me free will to
make whatever plans I choose. Before I was saved, I tried

to control my steps, but when God changed my heart, I realized the tremendous freedom of knowing that all my plans fit perfectly into His plan.

We visited Israel once and had the privilege of walking where Jesus walked. This experience has made the Bible even more instructive and real for us each time we have read it through. Our trip to Israel imprinted upon our hearts that the hands of Jesus are always holding ours as we walk the path He also walked, a path He has set before us.

God has a plan for every phase of your life's journey, too. When you arrive at one of life's inevitable crossroads, that's precisely the moment you should turn your thoughts and prayers toward Him. When you do, He will make Himself known to you in a time and manner of His choosing. God will guide your steps. Your task, simply put, is to let Him.

God is our greatest refuge. When every earthly support system fails, remember that God remains steadfast, and His love remains unchanged. When we encounter life's inevitable disappointments and setbacks, God remains faithful. When we suffer losses that leave us heartbroken, God is always with us, always ready to respond to our prayers, always working in our midst, always able to turn earthly tragedies into eternal triumphs.

LIGHT FOR OUR PATH FROM GOD'S WORD

I know, O Lord, that the way of man is not in himself, that it is not in man who walks to direct his steps.

Jeremiah 10:23 ESV

It is God who is at work in you, both to will and to work for His good pleasure.

Philippians 2:13 NASB

The Lord will perfect that which concerns me; Your mercy, O Lord, endures forever.

Psalm 138:8 NKJV

For it was You who created my inward parts; You knit me together in my mother's womb. I will praise You because I have been remarkably and wonderfully made. Your works are wonderful, and I know this very well. . . . Your eyes saw me when I was formless; all my days were written in Your book and planned before a single one of them began

Psalm 139:13-14, 16 HCSB

Well done, good and faithful servant. You have been faithful over a little; I will set you over much. Enter into the joy of your master.

Matthew 25:21 ESV

MORE IMPORTANT IDEAS ABOUT
GOD'S PLAN FOR YOU

I don't doubt that the Holy Spirit guides your decisions from within when you make them with the intention of pleasing God. The error would be to think that He speaks only within, whereas in reality He speaks also through Scripture, the Church, Christian friends, and books.

C. S. Lewis

God has a course mapped out for your life, and all the inadequacies in the world will not change His mind. He will be with you every step of the way. And though it may take time, He has a celebration planned for when you cross over the "Red Seas" of your life.

Charles Swindoll

If you believe in a God who controls the big things, you have to believe in a God who controls the little things. It is we, of course, to whom things look "little" or "big."

Elisabeth Elliot

God has a plan for the life of every Christian. Every circumstance, every turn of destiny, all things work together for your good and for His glory.

Billy Graham

Fear not, for I have redeemed you;
I have called you by your name; you are Mine.
When you pass through the waters,
I will be with you; and through the rivers,
they shall not overflow you.
When you walk through the fire,
you shall not be burned,
nor shall the flame scorch you.
For I am the Lord your God,
the Holy One of Israel, your Savior.

—

Isaiah 43:1-3 NKJV

GINI'S JOURNEY

A Journey of Faith

Gini and I have used the phrase, "We are but strangers and aliens—sojourners and exiles—on this earth." We know that our life together is a short journey begun, choreographed, and completed by the Lord, whose purposes we seek to accomplish along the way.

In the book of Hebrews, we are reminded that Abraham, when called by God, obeyed without question. Abraham's obedience was a natural outgrowth of his faith in the Lord:

> By <u>faith</u> Abraham obeyed when he was called to go out to a place that he was to receive as an inheritance. And he went out, not knowing where he was going. By <u>faith</u> he went to live in the land of promise, as in a foreign land, living in tents with Isaac and Jacob, heirs with him of the same promise. For he was looking forward to the city that has foundations, whose designer and builder is God. By <u>faith</u> Sarah herself received power to conceive, even when she was past the age, since she considered him faithful who had promised. Therefore from one man, and him as good as dead, were born descendants as many as the stars of heaven

and as many as the innumerable grains of sand by the seashore.

These all died in faith, not having received the things promised, but having seen them and greeted them from afar, and having acknowledged that they were strangers and exiles on the earth. For people who speak thus make it clear that they are seeking a homeland. If they had been thinking of that land from which they had gone out, they would have had opportunity to return. But as it is, they desire a better country, that is, a heavenly one. Therefore God is not ashamed to be called their God, for he has prepared for them a city.

Hebrews 11:8-16 ESV

Gini's life continues to be a journey of faith, and the peace that she feels is real. She knows that she is destined for a homeland that is far better than the one she inhabits now. Today, she is a sojourner in a foreign land, trekking day by day toward her heavenly destination prepared by her Lord.

Gini is homeward bound, more certain than ever of her destination. She has her eyes set on the goal before her, the goal of hearing God say, "Well done, good and faithful servant."

CHAPTER 3

~

Trusting God's Word

But He answered, "It is written:
Man must not live on bread alone, but on every word
that comes from the mouth of God."

—

Matthew 4:4 HCSB

A LESSON FOR THE JOURNEY

~

God has given you a roadmap for your journey.
That roadmap is the Holy Bible.

We often utilize GPS technology for travel. Spiritually we might say those letters stand for *God's Plan is Sure!* God has given us the Bible, and He intends for us to use His holy Word as a guidebook for life here on earth *and* to prepare us for life eternal in heaven. Although we depend on the Holy Spirit to help us understand and interpret it, how we choose to use that guidebook is entirely up to us. We can read it, treasure it, trust it, and follow its instructions, or we can ignore it. That choice is ours, and so, of course, are the consequences.

Gini and I have chosen to read the Bible together. In fact, we have read it from beginning to end each year for the last 25 years. And, during the majority of those years, we have held weekly "read through the Bible" meetings at Sunday school and/or in our home. Along the way, we have discovered, time and again, that God's Word is, indeed, "a light unto our path." It is both a light to our steps (one at a time) and a lamp to our path (leading us to Him, homeward, to heaven). The Bible will light your path, too, if you read it carefully and often.

God has made promises to mankind and to you. God's promises never fail and they never grow old. I pray that you will trust those promises. And, when God proves Himself time and again, share them with your family, with your friends, and with the world.

Is God's Word a lamp that guides your path? Is God's Word your indispensable GPS for everyday living, or is it relegated to Sunday morning services? Do you read the Bible faithfully or sporadically? The answers to these questions will determine the direction of your thoughts, the direction of your day, and the direction of your life.

God's Word can be a roadmap to a place of righteousness and abundance. Make it your roadmap. God's wisdom can be a light to guide your steps. Use it as your light today, tomorrow, and every day of your life—and then walk confidently in the footsteps of God's only begotten Son.

Heaven and earth will pass away,
but my words will never pass away.

—

Matthew 24:35 NIV

LIGHT FOR OUR PATH FROM GOD'S WORD

But the Helper, the Holy Spirit, whom the Father will send in My name, He will teach you all things and bring to your remembrance all that I have said to you.

John 14:26 ESV

Every word of God is pure: he is a shield unto them that put their trust in him.

Proverbs 30:5 KJV

Blessed are those who hunger and thirst for righteousness, for they will be filled.

Matthew 5:6 NIV

For the word of God is quick, and powerful, and sharper than any two-edged sword, piercing even to the dividing asunder of soul and spirit, and of the joints and marrow, and is a discerner of the thoughts and intents of the heart.

Hebrews 4:12 KJV

You, however, continue in the things you have learned and become convinced of, knowing from whom you have learned them, and that from childhood you have known the sacred writings which are able to give you the wisdom that leads to salvation through faith which is in Christ Jesus.

2 Timothy 3:14-15 NASB

MORE IMPORTANT IDEAS ABOUT GOD'S WORD

The Bible is God's Word, given to us by God Himself so we can know Him and His will for our lives.

Billy Graham

Nobody ever outgrows Scripture; the book widens and deepens with our years.

C. H. Spurgeon

God's voice isn't all that difficult to hear. He sometimes shouts through our pain, whispers to us while we're relaxing on vacation, occasionally, He sings to us in a song, and warns us through the sixty-six books of His written Word. It's right there, ink on paper. Count on it—that book will never lead you astray.

Charles Swindoll

You should not believe your conscience and your feelings more than the word which the Lord who receives sinners preaches to you.

Martin Luther

The Gospel is not so much a demand as it is an offer, an offer of new life to man by the grace of God.

E. Stanley Jones

We are being transformed and renewed
by the powerful Word of God.
His Word causes us to know and
obey the truth, from the heart;
and for the purpose of sharing that truth.

—

Gini Baillie Bible note at John 17:17

GINI'S JOURNEY

Genuine Genealogy

When Gini and I were married, all eight of our grandparents were still alive. We discussed family connections with each grandparent and collected stories and pictures. Not surprisingly, we became interested in genealogy.

In 1978, after 15 years of marriage, Gini and I went on a mission trip to Korea. During that month, the Lord showed us that *we* were not in charge of our lives—*He* is. Before that mission trip, Gini and I had tried to be good people. We were nominally going to church, yet had only a passing acquaintance with Jesus.

In Korea, everything changed when we came to trust Christ as our Lord and Savior.

Through years of Bible study—and after countless attempts to applying God's Word to the everyday realities of our lives—we realized that our *true* genealogy is this: we have been adopted, as daughter and son, by our loving Heavenly Father.

Gini and I raised three biological daughters. God has blessed us with eight grandchildren who all profess Christ as Lord and Savior. We also raised four foster boys who were part of a family of eight children (two girls, six boys). We have had all those children in our home many times since. So, we now have seven additional grandchildren from our foster sons. We also have a large spiritual family of believers in the many places we have lived and in the many churches with which we have worshipped. These people have become our sisters, brothers, sons, and daughters.

Our biological, foster, and spiritual children and grandchildren reflect Gini's life verse, 3 John 4: "I have no greater joy than to hear that my children are walking in the truth." Our children are grateful for the godly heritage they have received, for which we give God the glory. Our genuine genealogy is a spiritual one.

Finally, brethren, whatever is true, whatever is honorable, whatever is right, whatever is pure, whatever is lovely, whatever is of good repute, if there is any excellence and if anything worthy of praise, dwell on these things. The things you have learned and received and heard and seen in me, practice these things, and the God of peace will be with you.

—

Philippians 4:8-9 NASB

CHAPTER 4

Overcoming the Shock

These things I have spoken to you, that in Me you
may have peace. In the world you will have tribulation;
but be of good cheer, I have overcome the world.

—

John 16:33 NKJV

A LESSON FOR THE JOURNEY

When your world spins out of control,
God is still in charge.

I n the spring of 2011, Gini began experiencing physical symptoms that told us something wasn't right. So, we made an appointment with Gini's doctor and, on April 18th, she went in for testing. Initially, we were concerned that Gini had experienced a mild stroke, but an MRI revealed a diagnosis that was even more devastating: brain cancer.

In an instant, our world was turned upside down. Below is a portion of the e-mail I sent to family and friends:

OUR WORLD IS TURNED UPSIDE DOWN!

The events of Monday started with a doctor's appointment that suggested the symptoms might be something in the brain and probably a small stroke. Then an MRI at noon that revealed a 2½ inch tumor in her right frontal brain area that is probably a high grade glioma known as Glioblastoma multiforme.

Our world changed upside-down in less than 1 hour. But the Lord is faithful and gives us the comfort, peace, and strength to go through each day and trial. Truly, "In his heart man makes his plans, but the Lord guides and directs each step" (Proverbs 16:9). This is my life verse which has a new twist today, but still is just as true as ever!

To our God, who hung the stars in space and created all things and has a perfect plan, neither a small stroke nor a brain tumor was unknown to Him. Jesus, who suffered for us and who walked up the hill to Golgotha, also walks with us through this journey.

Perhaps you have picked up this book during a time of personal crisis. If so, you know from experience that when adversity arrives with little warning, the shockwaves can be intense. But even if you're still numb from the pain of a recent trauma, don't despair. Instead, look upon your experience as an opportunity to rely upon God completely and without reservation. Your Heavenly Father is trustworthy. He loves you, and He is in control. Yours is not a distant protector; God isn't just near, He is here. In your very room! And He is watching over your every step.

I sought the Lord, and He answered me
and delivered me from all my fears.

—

Psalm 34:4 HCSB

LIGHT FOR OUR PATH FROM GOD'S WORD

When they had preached the gospel to that city and had made many disciples, they returned to Lystra and to Iconium and to Antioch, strengthening the souls of the disciples, encouraging them to continue in the faith, and saying that through many tribulations we must enter the kingdom of God.

Acts 14:21-22 ESV

Blessed are you who hunger now, for you shall be satisfied. Blessed are you who weep now, for you shall laugh.

Luke 6:21 NASB

For God hath not given us the spirit of fear; but of power, and of love, and of a sound mind.

2 Timothy 1:7 KJV

Fear not, for I am with you; be not dismayed, for I am your God. I will strengthen you, yes, I will help you, I will uphold you with My righteous right hand.

Isaiah 41:10 NKJV

For where two or three have gathered together in My name, I am there in their midst.

Matthew 18:20 NASB

MORE IMPORTANT IDEAS ABOUT
OVERCOMING FEAR AND TRAUMA

I pray that God will convince you of your security in Christ. I pray that he will remind you that your name is engraved on his hands. I pray that you will hear him whisper, "So do not fear, for I am with you."

C. H. Spurgeon

Contentment is trusting God even when things seem out of control.

Charles Stanley

Fear and doubt are conquered by a faith that rejoices. And faith can rejoice because the promises of God are as certain as God Himself.

Kay Arthur

Jesus came treading the waves; and so he puts all the swelling tumults of life under his feet. Christians: why be afraid?

St. Augustine

We must, without apology, without fear, without ceasing, preach and practice our beliefs, carrying them out to the point of suffering.

R. G. Lee

GINI'S JOURNEY

Turning Everything Over to Him

Below is Gini's e-mail to family and friends on April 18, 2011, the day of her diagnosis.

Thank you so much for your love and prayers. I saw doctors from 9:30 until 5:30 today and had an MRI of my brain. Initially everyone was thinking a TIA (small stroke), but it turns out that I have a brain tumor. I'm going into the hospital in a few minutes so they can start IV steroids to try to get the swelling down. Dr. MacDonald (Neurosurgeon) had a cancelation for tomorrow so he will do surgery late tomorrow afternoon (4 or 5ish since I'm a "work in"). It's about 2½" in diameter and is in my right frontal lobe thus affecting my balance, etc.—especially the left side. I'll probably be in the hospital for 4 or 5 days. Our girls are planning to come ASAP, although I don't think the surgery itself is life-threatening. I may be sporting a new hair "do" for Easter (if I'm out of the hospital by then). My "room" will be in Neurosurgical ICU so it may be just as well not to have visitors until I get home as visiting is restricted somewhat. I know y'all love me/us and will be praying. Thank you again for that as the Lord is the One who gets us through the trials we must face!

As you can see from this e-mail, Gini had—and still has—a single-minded and complete trust in the Lord. She knows that her Father is in charge of all things and that He will protect and deliver her today, tomorrow, and forever. It is not a worldly faith with many choices of what to believe or many things to trust. Rather, it is a faith that has only one choice to believe in and only one thing to trust completely: a Sovereign God, in control of every detail of our lives.

Because of her faith, Gini has continued to experience "the peace that passes all understanding," even during some of the darkest days of her illness. You, too, can experience the peace that is promised in God's Word. You'll partake of that peace when you finally decide to turn everything—not *some* things, not *most* things . . . *everything*—over to Him.

Turning things over to God isn't a one-time event. You must learn to depend upon Him every day, availing yourself of His strength moment by moment, praying often and listening carefully. When you do, you'll discover that the initial shock of pain, grief, tears, and fears, like everything else on this earth, is temporary. Bible verses and songs, placed in your mind and heart, can help you through the shock. A verse from one such song to sing is: "I need Thee every hour, stay Thou nearby; temptations lose their power when Thou art nigh." God's plan is perfect. One day, He will wipe away every tear and make all things new.

I have found the perfect antidote for fear.
Whenever it sticks up its ugly face,
I defeat it with prayer.

—

Dale Evans Rogers

CHAPTER 5

What Doesn't Change

For I am the Lord, I do not change.

—

Malachi 3:6 NKJV

A LESSON FOR THE JOURNEY

When everything else in your life seems
to be spinning out of control,
one thing remains unchanged: God.

Our world is in a constant state of flux, and so are our lives. Because we continually encounter new circumstances, we are always in a state of "becoming," always adapting to ever-changing conditions. Sometimes, the changes we encounter are slow and subtle, so we hardly notice them. On other occasions, the changes are swift, harsh, and difficult to accept.

On April 18th, 2011, I felt like clawing at the ground and tearing my clothes as our world seemed to be spinning out of control. After Gini's MRI, our doctor made a dire diagnosis: glioblastoma of the brain. As a pathologist who had made this diagnosis many times, I knew what this diagnosis meant, and I understood the deadly implications of a tumor with "fingers" extending into the nearby normal brain, such that it cannot be completely removed.

My thoughts began to swirl. I could tell that Gini was scanning my face, trying to determine what I knew about her condition. And what I knew was horrifying: sitting there looking at Gini's beautiful face and eyes, I knew that just beyond them was a large and deadly tumor in the front of her brain. This knowledge was almost too much for me to take in.

What about the plans we had made? What about our dreams of sitting on the porch until we were 80, or continuing to go on special mission trips together? What about the joys of spending time with our family and friends?

Could all these things really be coming to an end in just a few months? I had so many unanswered questions, and I felt overwhelmed.

All of us must endure life-altering personal losses that leave us heartbroken. When we do, our Heavenly Father stands ready to comfort us and to guide us. He is, indeed, the "steadfast anchor of the soul," an anchor that always holds.

In her hymn "'Tis Well with Me," Fanny Crosby wrote,

My hope has found an anchor, a sure abiding home,
Upon the Rock of Ages, where storms can never come.
And though I hear the tumult of ocean surges swell,
My soul is calm and peaceful. 'Tis well with me, 'tis well.

These words remind us that God is, indeed, a refuge from the storms of life. He is a source of peace when we are crushed; He is a source of courage when we are afraid.

Although God has guided you through many struggles in the past, you may still find your faith stretched to the limit whenever you encounter adversity, uncertainty, or declining health. But the good news is this: Even though your circumstances may change, God's love for you does not. Your plans, your abilities, and your priorities will change, but God's unchanging plan for your life will not change!

Is the world spinning a little too fast for your liking? Are you facing difficult circumstances or physical hardships? If so, please remember that God is far bigger than any challenge you face. Even if there seems, to you, no way out, the Lord can find a way.

So today, instead of fretting about life's inevitable setbacks, put your faith in the Father and His only begotten Son. Seek protection from the One who cannot be moved.

The same God who created the universe will protect you if you ask Him . . . so ask Him . . . and then serve a good and Sovereign God, wherever you are planted, with willing hands and a trusting heart.

The Lord's lovingkindnesses indeed never cease,
for His compassions never fail.
They are new every morning.
Great is Thy faithfulness.

—

Lamentations 3:22-23 NASB

LIGHT FOR OUR PATH FROM GOD'S WORD

I waited patiently for the Lord, and He turned to me and heard my cry for help. He brought me up from a desolate pit, out of the muddy clay, and set my feet on a rock, making my steps secure. He put a new song in my mouth, a hymn of praise to our God.

Psalm 40:1-3 HCSB

The LORD is my strength and song, and He has become my salvation.

Exodus 15:2 NASB

Be still, and know that I am God.

Psalm 46:10 NKJV

No temptation has overtaken you that is not common to man. God is faithful, and he will not let you be tempted beyond your ability, but with the temptation he will also provide the way of escape, that you may be able to endure it.

1 Corinthians 10:33 ESV

Yet once more I will shake . . . indicates the removal of things that are shaken—that is, things that have been made—in order that the things that cannot be shaken may remain.

Hebrews 12:26-27 ESV

MORE IMPORTANT IDEAS ABOUT CHANGE
AND SPIRITUAL GROWTH

Nothing has any power to alter a man save the incoming of the life of Jesus.

Oswald Chambers

What we have once enjoyed and deeply loved we can never lose, for all that we love deeply becomes a part of us.

Helen Keller

Keep your face upturned to Christ as the flowers do to the sun. Look, and your soul shall live and grow.

Hannah Whitall Smith

It is tempting to imagine that, given a different lot in life, circumstances other than those in which we find ourselves, we would make much greater strides in holiness. The truth is that the place where we are is God's schoolroom, not somewhere else. Here we may be conformed to the likeness of Christ.

Elisabeth Elliot

Sometimes your medicine bottle says, "Shake well before using." That is what God has to do with some of his people. He has to shake them well before they are useable.

Vance Havner

GINI'S JOURNEY

Growing in Grace . . .
Moment by Moment

After Gini's recovery from surgery and from her initial treatments, we were in a bit of a struggle about all the changes that had occurred. We could have despaired, or we could have gotten angry at God. But we refused to give in to these temptations.

At times, we certainly *did* wonder whether God *really* cared—but we continued to remind ourselves that His love endures forever. So, instead of protesting against God's will, Gini and I asked Him what He would have us do with the remainder of our days on this earth.

In spite of physical impediments that were new to her, Gini still believed that she could make a difference for the Lord. In time, she began ministering to people by phone and by emails that I helped her compose. Amazingly, Gini still welcomed visitors into our home. And even when words failed her, she quickly learned that her smile could speak volumes about her trust in God Almighty, whose plan for her life was and continues to be unchanged.

Today, despite her physical and mental changes, Gini continues to share (although a bit differently) the knowledge and application of the Bible that the Lord has taught her. What a joy it is for her to realize that she can still minister to others despite the hardships she endures. Those whom she taught through the years are now coming to share God's truths and promises with her, giving encouragement to each other in the unchanging goal to glorify God in every thought, word, and deed.

In the closing words of his second letter, Peter had the following advice: "But grow in the grace and knowledge of our Lord and Savior Jesus Christ. To Him be the glory both now and to the day of eternity. Amen."

I have watched Gini continue to grow in grace moment by moment, day by day. What an inspiration she is to me, to my family, and to our friends.

Our experiences have taught Gini and me this important lesson: We can grow *wherever* we are planted . . . *or* transplanted! Our prayer for you is that though the storms of change assail you greatly, you will see how God has changed you and continues to use you for His unchanging plan.

CHAPTER 6

Rest in the Lord

*Do not be anxious about anything, but in everything
by prayer and supplication with thanksgiving let your
requests be made known to God. And the peace of God,
which surpasses all understanding, will guard
your hearts and your minds in Christ Jesus.*

—

Philippians 4:6-7 ESV

A LESSON FOR THE JOURNEY

When you face challenges that make you
anxious or fearful, remember that God's peace
is always available to you.

Sometimes, we encounter hardships that seem almost too much to bear. Thankfully, none of us need to carry our burdens alone. Our Heavenly Father is always willing to help us shoulder the weight. When we ask for His help, He does not withhold it. In fact, He does the opposite. When we yield to Him as our Sovereign Lord, He carries the heaviest part of the load.

When I asked Gini for her best advice about confronting the inevitability of death, her response was as simple as it was profound. She said, "Rest in the Lord." And, that's precisely what she's done.

The English pastor C. H. Spurgeon noted, "Any man can sing in the day. It is easy to sing when we can read the notes by daylight, but he is the skillful singer who can sing when there is not a ray of light by which to read. Songs in the night come only from God; they are not in the power of man."

After her surgery, Gini had times that she could not think or speak coherently, but when we would interrupt her with "I love you", she would respond with "I love you too!" And, we discovered that if we started a verse of scripture that she knew by memory, she would complete it. She could also sing along with us when we sang her favorite hymns.

Over her lifetime, Gini had created a storehouse of memorized scripture and songs. When her mind was confused in the midst of radiation and chemo, such that thoughts and words were difficult, she could call upon those memories and be comforted. Amazingly, Gini could still sing clearly when just the music was played for her, and even sing in the middle of the night. God truly does provide for us, even in our sleep!

During the darker days of life, we are wise to remember that God is with us always and that He offers us His gifts of comfort, assurance, and peace—our task, of course, is to accept these gifts, use them, and be ever grateful.

God's promises never fail. As Spurgeon also observed, "A promise from God may very instructively be compared to a check payable to you. It is given to the believer with the view of bestowing upon him some good thing. It is not meant that he should read it over comfortably, and then have done with it. No, he is to treat the promise as a reality, as a man treats a check." There is always a large balance credited to our account, so draw heavily from God's resources!

When we trust in God's promises, the world becomes a less frightening place. Then, with God's love in our hearts, we are prepared to tackle our earthly challenges with courage, determination, and faith. Because our God is forever trustworthy, we can rest in Him.

LIGHT FOR OUR PATH FROM GOD'S WORD

Let us hold fast the confession of our hope without wavering, for He who promised is faithful.

Hebrews 10:23 NASB

O Lord, my heart is not proud, nor my eyes haughty; nor do I involve myself in great matters, or in things too difficult for me. Surely I have composed and quieted my soul; like a weaned child rests against his mother, my soul is like a weaned child within me. O Israel, hope in the Lord from this time forth and forever.

Psalm 131 NASB

Peace I leave with you, my peace I give unto you: not as the world giveth, give I unto you. Let not your heart be troubled, neither let it be afraid.

John 14:27 KJV

Therefore, since we have so great a cloud of witnesses surrounding us, let us also lay aside every encumbrance and the sin which so easily entangles us, and let us run with endurance the race that is set before us, fixing our eyes on Jesus, the author and perfecter of faith.

Hebrews 12:1-2 NASB
(which Gini has now handwritten for each grandchild)

MORE IMPORTANT IDEAS ABOUT GOD'S PEACE

We're prone to want God to change our circumstances, but He wants to change our character. We think that peace comes from the outside in, but it comes from the inside out.

Warren Wiersbe

Thou hast formed us for Thyself, and our hearts are restless till they find rest in Thee.

St. Augustine

Peace is the deepest thing a human personality can know; it is almighty.

Oswald Chambers

What peace can they have who are not at peace with God?

Matthew Henry

The better acquainted you become with God, the less tensions you feel and the more peace you possess.

Charles Allen

The peace that Jesus gives is never engineered by circumstances on the outside.

Oswald Chambers

Jesus did not promise to change
the circumstances around us.
He promised great peace and
pure joy to those who would learn
to believe that God
actually controls all things.

—

Corrie ten Boom

GINI'S JOURNEY

Called Off the Bench

When Gini received her diagnosis on that Monday in April, our world suddenly changed. She was promptly treated with large doses of steroids to prevent brain swelling and then operated on to remove a 2½ inch tumor.

Immediately, our friends and relatives began to surround us with God's love and comfort. It would have been an overwhelming task to keep our friends all over the world informed, but the Lord made it possible through the technology CaringBridge.org. It was on the CaringBridge site that I began the journaling process that has described Gini's journey.

This trial in Gini's life has thrust both of us out of the stands and onto the playing field with the Lord's playbook, not ours. We have the blessed opportunity to follow His coaching and play-calling, knowing that He is also the referee and the time keeper! The plays He chooses may result in losses or gains, but no matter. We must run with endurance to the goal, making meaningful interaction with all our teammates and opponents, as well as the fans in the stands.

The Lord has chosen to grant us time to be a meaningful witness for Him, but in totally different and unexpected ways. It truly is His game through and through—not ours! So, we endeavor that each day be "game day" as we allow His peace to rule in our hearts.

Our prayer for you is that you will follow His leading in faith, and see this as truly resting in God's promises and experiencing His peace. Remember that God's love endures forever. And, don't forget that He is trustworthy today, tomorrow, and forever.

And let the peace of God rule in your hearts . . . and be ye thankful.

—

Colossians 3:15 KJV

CHAPTER 7

Discovering God's Purpose

It is God who is at work in you,
both to will and to work for His good pleasure.

—

Philippians 2:13 NASB

A LESSON FOR THE JOURNEY

God uses ordinary people to accomplish
extraordinary things.

We live in a world populated by ordinary people. More often than not, we human beings are used by the Lord to accomplish His purposes through ordinary means, not miraculous ones.

Of course, we all possess various talents, gifted by the Lord. And, we are all responsible for using those talents to the best of our abilities. But even when we do our best, we can accomplish little by ourselves. To accomplish the miraculous, we need God and His guidance.

Gini has mentored many young women by investing countless hours in frank discussions, heartfelt prayers, and serious Bible study, starting with our daughters, Becky, Kim, and Heather. Then names like Stacy, Christie, Ann-Janette, Marcia, and Anna come to mind, but these are just a few of the younger women who have been blessed by Gini's ministry. The Lord is using Gini—an ordinary woman, an ordinary wife, an ordinary mother, and an ordinary grandmother—in extraordinary ways. And, God wants to use you, too, for the glory of His kingdom.

If you're experiencing tough times, you may be asking yourself, "What does God want me to do next?" Perhaps you're pondering your future, uncertain of your plans, unsure of your next step. But even if you don't have a clear plan for the next phase of your life's journey, you may rest assured that God does.

God has a plan for the universe, and He has a plan

for you. He understands that plan as thoroughly and completely as He knows you. As you seek God's will earnestly and prayerfully, He will make His plans known to you in His own time and in His own way. Even though you don't know *where* your journey will lead, or *when* your journey on this earth will end, you must trust the One who has planned that journey because He is faithful.

When you turn things over to the Lord—and when you earnestly seek to follow in the footsteps of His Son— you should expect God to use you, an "ordinary" person, to do "extraordinary" things.

Sometimes, God's plans and purposes may seem unmistakably clear to you. If so, push ahead. But other times, He may lead you through the wilderness before He directs you to the Promised Land. So be patient and keep seeking His will for your life. When you do, you'll be amazed at the marvelous things that an all-powerful, all-knowing God can do through you.

LIGHT FOR OUR PATH FROM GOD'S WORD

I will instruct you and teach you in the way you should go; I will counsel you with my eye upon you.

Psalm 32:8 ESV

The Lord is my chosen portion and my cup; you hold my lot. The lines have fallen for me in pleasant places; indeed, I have a beautiful inheritance. I bless the Lord who gives me counsel; in the night also my heart instructs me. I have set the Lord always before me; because he is at my right hand, I shall not be shaken.

Psalm 16:5-8 ESV

For consider your calling, brothers: not many of you were wise according to worldly standards, not many were powerful, not many were of noble birth. But God chose what is foolish in the world to shame the wise; God chose what is weak in the world to shame the strong; God chose what is low and despised in the world, even things that are not, to bring to nothing things that are, so that no human being might boast in the presence of God.

1 Corinthians 1:26-29 ESV

And we know that God causes all things to work together for good to those who love God, to those who are called according to His purpose.

Romans 8:28 NASB

MORE IMPORTANT IDEAS ABOUT
GOD'S PEOPLE ON THE ROAD:
FINDING PURPOSE

Without God, life has no purpose, and without purpose, life has no meaning.

Rick Warren

Christian discipleship is a process of paying more and more attention to God's righteousness and less and less attention to our own; finding the meaning of our lives not by probing our moods and motives and morals, but by believing in God's will and purposes; making a map of the faithfulness of God, not charting the rise and fall of our enthusiasms.

Eugene Peterson

Whatever purpose motivates your life, it must be something big enough and grand enough to make the investment worthwhile.

Warren Wiersbe

We must always invite Jesus to be the navigator of our plans, desires, wills, and emotions, for He is the way, the truth, and the life.

Bill Bright

For I know the plans I have for you,
declares the Lord, plans for welfare
and not for evil, to give you
a future and a hope.

—

Jeremiah 29:11 ESV

GINI'S JOURNEY

Mentoring

Before her diagnosis, Gini was an ordinary teacher and counselor, made extraordinary by the Lord. She taught Sunday school, led Bible studies, and mentored many young women. One of those women is named Christy. Below are excerpts from a note Christy wrote to Gini after Gini's surgery.

Dear Gini,

I had been praying for a mentor for years before I asked you that day after church. I was just talking about my desire to have a mentor, and I didn't know you very well at the time, but you immediately said, "I'll do it!"

I love your willingness to give of yourself to others. I remember going to your house on many occasions. You would just make tea and listen to me. I really needed that. And, you were never shy about sharing the gospel.

I am so thankful for what we've shared in this life together, and I love you very much.

Christy

Gini still inspires others, but now she ministers in new ways. Despite the heart-wrenching trials she's endured, she continues to accomplish God's purposes through her courage, through her attitude, through her example, through her faith, and, of course, through her smile.

Gini and I pray that the Lord will use your "ordinary" journey to accomplish mighty and "extraordinary" things. And we pray that He would have you contemplate your own life—and its end—so that you will find purpose in the "here and now," as well as the grace to finish well.

Be strong and courageous and do it.
Do not be afraid and do not be dismayed,
for the Lord God, even my God, is with you.
He will not leave you or forsake you,
until all the work for the service of the house
of the Lord is finished.

—

1 Chronicles 28:20 ESV

CHAPTER 8

— ✤ —

Trust in the Lord

*Trust the Lord your God with all your heart
and lean not on your own understanding;
in all your ways acknowledge him,
and he will make your paths straight.*

—

Proverbs 3:5-6 NIV

A LESSON FOR THE JOURNEY

— ✤ —

It's tempting to trust the world's wisdom,
but it is often wrong to do so.
Don't put your faith in *worldly* wisdom;
instead, trust God's wisdom.

Wisdom comes in at least two varieties: the world's version and God's. The wisdom of God often seems foolish to man. But mankind's wisdom is also foolishness to God. While God's wisdom never fails, worldly wisdom is not so. When the storms of life beat down upon us, the world's wisdom simply doesn't hold up.

What does it look like to trust God as your wife is going in for brain surgery? What does it look like to trust God as you want to do things for her you've never had to do before, like putting on lipstick and rouge, earrings, putting on her clothes, taking her into the women's bathroom when traveling, and other things you do not do well? What does it look like to trust God as you contemplate— and journey toward—her death?

As I ponder these questions, I realize that the Lord is asking me to bring up from the depths of my heart things that I simply don't have answers to. He's asking me to prove that I can trust Him in *all* things: not a few specific things, and not just the things I feel comfortable dealing with. The Lord is asking me to trust Him in every aspect of my life.

One of the women who helped in our home was Anna, a college student. She helped for two summers and occasionally during the school year. She saw Gini's and my relationship, and she saw a trust in the Lord that made an impression upon her. Anna wrote a note that described what she saw: a real Christian husband and wife dealing with a very difficult trial and trusting Him completely in everything, all day, every day. Here's a portion of that note:

"I was with the Baillies often enough and long enough to know that they were not faking things in front of me—they had real trust. I desire to have that same trust relationship and am thankful to the Lord for providing real people as an example."

Wow! I read those words and realize how the Lord is working through both Gini and myself in very difficult times for His glory. Many, many times, I have felt like I was at the end of my rope, really struggling with everything that was—and still is—occurring. I am thankful that the Lord continues to be faithful to us as we put ourselves in His hands.

Today provides another opportunity for you to choose between the world's wisdom and God's. Is there anything specific right now that the Lord is asking you to trust Him with that you are hesitant or unwilling to do? At this very moment, you can place your trust in the Father's promises as you place your eternal fate in the loving hands of His Son. If you *do*, you will be secure, no matter how dire your circumstances.

So, here is my message, my prayer, and my hope for you: I pray that you will be resolute in seeing and savoring the Savior, and that you will put your complete trust in Him all your days. And I pray that you will see the importance of God's Word and the need for His guidance in your every thought, word, and deed.

Today, as a gift to yourself and your loved ones, summon the courage to trust God's wisdom. Even if the path seems difficult, even if your heart is fearful, trust your Heavenly Father and follow Him. Trust Him with this very day and the rest of your life. Do His work, care for His children, and share His Good News. Let Him guide your steps. He will not lead you astray.

Those who trust in the Lord are like Mount Zion, which cannot be moved, but abides forever.

—

Psalm 125:1 ESV

LIGHT FOR OUR PATH FROM GOD'S WORD

"For My thoughts are not your thoughts, nor are your ways My ways," says the LORD. "For as the heavens are higher than the earth, so are My ways higher than your ways, and My thoughts than your thoughts."

Isaiah 55:8-9 NKJV

The fear of the Lord is the beginning of wisdom; a good understanding have all those who do His commandments. His praise endures forever.

Psalm 111:10 NKJV

Trust ye in the LORD for ever: for in the LORD JEHOVAH is everlasting strength.

Isaiah 26:4 KJV

The LORD is my rock, and my fortress, and my deliverer; my God, my strength, in whom I will trust....

Psalm 18:2 KJV

Everyone then who hears these words of mine and does them will be like a wise man who built his house on the rock. And the rain fell, and the floods came, and the winds blew and beat on that house, but it did not fall, because it had been founded on the rock.

Matthew 7:24–25 ESV

MORE IMPORTANT IDEAS ABOUT
TRUSTING GOD

Trusting in my own mental understanding becomes a hindrance to complete trust in God.

Oswald Chambers

God has proven himself as a faithful father. Now it falls to us to be trusting children.

Max Lucado

Are you serious about wanting God's guidance to become the person he wants you to be? The first step is to tell God that you know you can't manage your own life; that you need His help.

Catherine Marshall

Never be afraid to trust an unknown future to a known God.

Corrie ten Boom

If in everything you seek Jesus, you will doubtless find Him. But if you seek yourself, you will indeed find yourself, to your own ruin. For you do yourself more harm by not seeking Jesus than the whole world and all your enemies could do to you.

Thomas à Kempis

GINI'S JOURNEY

Accountable to Each Other

For over twenty years, Gini and I have been accountable to each other for a critically important task: reading the Bible and praying together day by day. As we have read through God's Word again and again, we've discovered it to be an invaluable tool as we strive to apply His teachings to the specific application of His will for our lives.

When it comes to studying the Bible and applying it to the details of everyday life, accountability is important. That's why Gini and I also led weekly Bible-study groups to discuss, to teach, and to be accountable to one another for the reading of God's Word.

The format for our group Bible readings was simple. We had a specific reading plan for each year, sometimes straight through and sometimes chronologically. Then, we met weekly to share what we had learned, while making sure that key points of God's message, and application to our lives, were not overlooked.

What a joy it is to be challenged to read through the Bible each year! So, our prayer for you is simple: We pray that your needs will be supplied by a daily reading from God's Word, and that you may also wonder anew at all that God has done for you.

On one occasion, we were studying the communion passage in 1 Corinthians 11: "Do this in remembrance of me." This passage teaches us to "remember" what the Lord did for us in the PAST by being born a man (in every sense except sin) and dying for us; then a "remembering" of what Christ is doing for us in the PRESENT (by being The Word and guiding us each step we take day by day); and a "remembering" the FUTURE, by trusting that He will come again to deliver us into the heavenly realm to spend eternity with, and worship, Him.

We all need to see the joy, the love, and the peace that comes from evaluating our past and its events. We need to see that the Lord is teaching, training, and working in us as we seek to live in the new life we have with Christ.

Storing up God's Word in your heart is very important. If you have never read through the Bible, we would strongly encourage you to do so. In order to read through the entire Bible in one year, you can read three to four chapters a day, which takes about 15 minutes. Or, you can read five chapters a day for five days of each week. For "first timers," I suggest a chronological reading plan. I also remind folks that if they get behind more than five days, they should just jump to the current day and continue reading. This strategy is based on the principle that you can easily eat one banana a day, but if you get behind and have 30 to eat in one day, it is very difficult!

CHAPTER 9

Encourage One Another

But encourage one another day after day,
as long as it is still called "Today," so that none of you
will be hardened by the deceitfulness of sin.

—

Hebrews 3:13 NASB

A LESSON FOR THE JOURNEY

God has placed fellow travelers along your path;
He wants you to strengthen your fellow travelers
and to be strengthened by them.

While Gini was in rehab, the Lord placed folks along my path at just the right time to provide opportunities for mutual encouragement. One such person was a cafeteria worker who cooked a different special pasta dish each day at the Duke Regional Hospital. Everybody called her "Mrs. T."

One day, I was running late; it was near the end of the serving hours, and Mrs. T had no line. So, I stepped up, asked her how she was doing, and she replied, "I'm blessed. What brings you here?"

I answered that the Lord had given us a great day, and that my wife had a brain tumor. I added that Gini was on the rehab floor.

Mrs. T quietly turned, reached for a paper towel, and handed it to me along with a ready pen. She asked me to write my wife's name so her church folks could pray for Gini. I did so and thanked Mrs. T for her encouragement, for her prayers, and for yet another plate of delicious pasta.

What server in a cafeteria line would keep a pen so handy if she did not also have a purpose in mind for its use? Mrs. T had prepared herself to serve her customers in more ways than one!

In the following two passages from John 4, we are told how Jesus revealed Himself to the woman from Samaria, and how He taught His disciples about spiritual sustenance:

A woman from Samaria came to draw water. Jesus said to her, "Give me a drink." (For his disciples had gone away into the city to buy food.) . . .

Jesus said to her, "Woman, believe me, the hour is coming when neither on this mountain nor in Jerusalem will you worship the Father. You worship what you do not know; we worship what we know, for salvation is from the Jews. But the hour is coming, and is now here, when the true worshipers will worship the Father in spirit and truth, for the Father is seeking such people to worship him. God is spirit, and those who worship him must worship in spirit and truth." The woman said to him, "I know that Messiah is coming (he who is called Christ). When he comes, he will tell us all things." Jesus said to her, "I who speak to you am he."

Just then his disciples came back. They marveled that he was talking with a woman, but no one said, "What do you seek?" or, "Why are you talking with her?" So the woman left her water jar and went away into town and said to the people, "Come, see a man who told me all that I ever did. Can this be the Christ?" They went out of the town and were coming to him.

Meanwhile the disciples were urging him, saying, "Rabbi, eat." But he said to them, "I have food to eat that you do not know about." So the disciples said to one another, "Has anyone brought him something to

eat?" Jesus said to them, "My food is to do the will
of him who sent me and to accomplish his work. Do
you not say, 'There are yet four months, then comes
the harvest'? Look, I tell you, lift up your eyes, and
see that the fields are white for harvest. Already the
one who reaps is receiving wages and gathering fruit
for eternal life, so that sower and reaper may rejoice
together. For here the saying holds true, 'One sows
and another reaps.' I sent you to reap that for which
you did not labor. Others have labored, and you have
entered into their labor."

John 4:7-8, 21-38 ESV

Christ's disciples had gone to the city to buy food, and
upon their return, they were somewhat puzzled that Jesus
would associate with a Samaritan. After the woman left,
the disciples urged Him to eat, but Jesus told them that He
had food they did not know about. Then, Christ taught
His disciples about *spiritual* nourishment.

As I thought about Mrs. T's encouraging words for me,
I realized that the Lord had allowed me to "digest" His provision of spiritual food that day *before* I ate a single bite of
lunch. Mrs. T's words and prayers were just what I needed
at that moment. I thanked God for the woman who no-
ticed people *without* Duke name tags and engaged them
quietly and gently.

But, the story didn't end there. After I finished lunch that day, I walked to the elevator and encountered a man who, like myself, had a temporary nametag, not the official Duke version. The man was carrying a take-away lunch box. He asked me to push number 5, which I knew to be the cardiac floor. I asked how he was doing, and he responded, "Not too good." He said that his father was on that floor.

So, remembering the kindness of Mrs. T, I passed along a portion of the encouragement she had just given to me. I promised to pray for the man's dad, and he seemed grateful. Then, as he reached his floor and walked off the elevator, I thanked the Lord for the opportunity to receive spiritual food *and* to give it away. And, I remembered that Gini often quoted, "We are just one beggar showing another beggar where to find bread."

LIGHT FOR OUR PATH FROM GOD'S WORD

Encourage each other. Live in harmony and peace. Then the God of love and peace will be with you.

2 Corinthians 13:11 NLT

Let the word of Christ dwell in you richly in all wisdom; teaching and admonishing one another in psalms and hymns and spiritual songs, singing with grace in your hearts to the Lord.

Colossians 3:16 KJV

Finally, all of you be of one mind, having compassion for one another; love as brothers, be tenderhearted, be courteous.

1 Peter 3:8 NKJV

Therefore encourage one another and build up one another, just as you also are doing.

1 Thessalonians 5:11 NASB

Let us hold fast the confession of our hope without wavering, for he who promised is faithful. And let us consider how to stir up one another to love and good works, not neglecting to meet together, as is the habit of some, but encouraging one another, and all the more as you see the Day drawing near.

Hebrews 10:23-25 ESV

MORE IMPORTANT IDEAS ABOUT THE POWER OF ENCOURAGEMENT

A single word, if spoken in a friendly spirit, may be sufficient to turn one from dangerous error.

Fanny Crosby

God grant that we may not hinder those who are battling their way slowly into the light.

Oswald Chambers

I would go to the deeps a hundred times to cheer a downcast spirit. It is good for me to have been afflicted, that I might know how to speak a word in season to one that is weary.

Charles Spurgeon

If I can put one touch of rosy sunset into the life of any man or woman, I shall feel that I have worked with God.

G. K. Chesterton

Christians are like the several flowers in a garden that have each of them the dew of heaven, which, being shaken with the wind, they let fall at each other's roots, whereby they are jointly nourished, and become nourishers of each other.

John Bunyan

GINI'S JOURNEY

Blessed Memory Verses

God's Word has the power to lift our spirits, even during life's darkest moments. That's one reason (but certainly not the only reason) that we're wise to commit verses to memory and place them securely in our hearts. One of our pastors, Patrick, told a short story to help make this point: If you bump a cup and there is nothing in it, nothing can spill. The cup can only spill what it contains. So, why not fill your cup with the Word, so that when you are bumped, His truth and His promises are what spills?

Before her illness, Gini had memorized countless verses and entire passages from the Bible, including the Sermon on the Mount. As one of several memory aids she utilized, she recorded her own voice and then listened to the passages again and again. She even listened as she fell asleep each night. Because she had recorded over two hours of Bible verses, Gini could start in a different place each evening.

Sometimes, Gini also listened to her recordings while she was walking alone. More than once she said, "Just think about it; you know the words to songs because you have listened to them over and over. The Israelites taught their children by singing some of the Psalms as they traveled along the road to Jerusalem."

After Gini's surgery, we were very thankful for her recordings. During the long nights in rehab, we played those verses back to her, so she could listen to God's promises spoken in her own voice. Today, Gini says that hearing God's Word continues to be a source of comfort and encouragement to her. We also believe that her recordings were a great help in the hospital when her thoughts were often confused.

Memorization was always harder for me than it was for Gini. Although I can usually remember where passages are located, and their principal meanings, I often fail to remember the exact wording of each verse. So, when Gini encouraged me to memorize scriptures, I was resistant, as were many others.

Gini insisted that memorizing verses might be one of the most important things I could do for myself, but I had the tendency to just say, "I just can't do that."

One day she challenged me by saying that I could remember what I was looking at under the microscope because I practiced all day, every day—so why, she asked, was I not "practicing" God's Word in the same way?

She also told one of our foster sons, who was trying to earn $25 for memorizing 17 verses, "You can remember who was the runner-up in the last five Super Bowls, so I know you can remember what is important to you."

It's obvious that when Gini thinks something is important, she doesn't beat around the bush. Instead, she's very bold and direct in her encouragements.

Gini encourages *you* to record your own version of favorite verses, for present and future reference. And, we both pray that you'll take her advice.

Carry each other's burdens,
and in this way you will fulfill the law of Christ.

—

Galatians 6:2 NIV

CHAPTER 10

Every Moment a Gift

To everything there is a season, and a time to every purpose under the heaven: A time to be born, and a time to die; a time to plant, and a time to pluck up that which is planted . . . A time to weep, and a time to laugh; a time to mourn, and a time to dance; A time to cast away stones, and a time to gather stones together; a time to embrace, and a time to refrain from embracing . . . A time to love, and a time to hate; a time of war, and a time of peace.

—

Ecclesiastes 3:1-8 KJV

A LESSON FOR THE JOURNEY

Time is a gift, and God's timing is perfect. On every stage of your journey—and on the great stage of life—you can trust Him completely.

Time is a gift of God. He created it; He ordered it to be, and He arranged it in His own perfect way. God orchestrates the use and the unfolding of time, all within His infinite, boundless eternity.

The Lord has put each of us on the stage of life and written a script that is uniquely ours. We are living in His Story. He directs the play. We have some freedom as actors, but only when permitted can we leave the stage. We follow the direction—and correction—of the Director for the ultimate result that He intends. As the play unfolds, we learn to see His boundaries as we study under, and follow, His teachings and experience His discipline.

An important element of our stewardship to God is the way that we, as His actors, choose to spend our time upon His stage. Each waking moment holds the potential to help a friend, to aid a stranger, to say a kind word, or to pray earnestly. Our challenge is to use our time wisely in the service of God's work and in accordance with His plan for our lives.

Are you trying to direct your own life? How are you choosing to spend the time that God has given you? Are you investing your life wisely or are you wasting precious days rushing here and there after the countless distractions and temptations that the world has to offer? With each sunset, we are one day closer to the moment of our departure from this earth.

As you establish priorities for your day and your life, remember that each new day is a special treasure of 86,400 moments we call seconds, to be savored and celebrated. If you are a Christian, you have much to celebrate and much to do. It's up to you to honor God for the gift of time by using that gift wisely.

Throughout our journey through this earthly life, God is molding us; we see His amazing purpose as He sovereignly orchestrates all the circumstances in our lives. During our own sufferings, Gini and I have been reminded time and time again that every day—*even* a day filled with hardship—is a treasure from above. And we have made up our minds to redeem that gift of precious time, as best we can, for as long as God gives us the seconds, hours, days, months, and years to discover His will and the strength to do it. We pray that you will trust and follow the Director.

I will repay you for the years the locusts have eaten.

—

Joel 2:25 NIV

LIGHT FOR OUR PATH FROM GOD'S WORD

So teach us to number our days, that we may gain a heart of wisdom.

Psalm 90:12 NKJV

Look carefully then how you walk, not as unwise but as wise, making the best use of the time, because the days are evil.

Ephesians 5:15-16 ESV

Therefore, preparing your minds for action, and being sober-minded, set your hope fully on the grace that will be brought to you at the revelation of Jesus Christ.

1 Peter 1:13 ESV

We must work the works of him who sent me while it is day; night is coming, when no one can work.

John 9:4 ESV

For it is God who works in you, both to will and to work for his good pleasure.

Philippians 2:13 ESV

I have told you these things, so that in me you may have peace. In this world you will have trouble. But take heart! I have overcome the world.

John 16:33 NIV

MORE IMPORTANT IDEAS ABOUT TREASURING—AND USING—EACH MOMENT

The whole essence of the spiritual life consists in recognizing the designs of God for us at the present moment.

Elisabeth Elliot

Live in such a way that any day would make a suitable capstone for life. Live so that you need not change your mode of living, even if your sudden departure were immediately predicted to you.

C. H. Spurgeon

Today is mine. Tomorrow is none of my business. If I peer anxiously into the fog of the future, I will strain my spiritual eyes so that I will not see clearly what is required of me now.

Elisabeth Elliot

I beg you do not squander life. And don't live for this world only.

Billy Graham

Fill the unforgiving minute with sixty seconds worth of distance run.

Rudyard Kipling

*But the path of the righteous is like
the light of dawn, that shines brighter
and brighter until the full day.*

—

Proverbs 4:18 NASB

Make the best use of your time—
of every moment.
Light given to you each day
by the Light of the world.

—

Gene Baillie Bible note at Proverbs 4:18

GINI'S JOURNEY

*Entrusting Each Moment
of Each Day to Him*

Below is a message from Anna, the daughter of a woman who had faithfully attended, and helped teach, many of the Bible-study groups led by Gini. Anna worked in our home often after Gini's surgery and her words serve as a reminder that we must trust the Father during good times *and* during trying times.

Before serving in the Baillies' home, I had emerged from a long period of doubt and anxiety. During this time, I had learned to claim righteousness in the blood of Christ alone, but I also had to rebuild my definition of "everyday trust."

My whole life, I had struggled with what it meant to "trust in the Lord." With all my pre-suppositions torn down, I began to watch the Baillies in their daily lives. Even though this trial surrounded their days like water threatening to engulf an island, I saw a thread of holy confidence in their countenances. I didn't see them pray elaborate prayers, weep on their knees, or spend hours in confession. What I did observe were conversations about God with a stranger at the grocery store, forgiveness of each other's failings, praise for the sunshine and singing birds, a subtle longing for heaven, and a meal for a visitor. Mrs. Baillie could hardly walk outside her home, but God was still touching hearts through her. Their no-frills, child-like faith astounded me.

Finally, I saw that I could let go of my self-made expectations and trust God to lead my day. I didn't have to cross the sea to find Christ at work. In fact, it was not about me at all. Seeing God use the Baillies right where they were, in the midst of cancer and pain, showed me the simplicity of trust. It opened my heart to the truth that God had planned opportunities to use me for His glory amid the daily grind. My perspective ratified, I came to understand that trust, for me, is knowing that my loving Shepherd will lead me in "paths of righteousness for His name's sake," as I simply put one foot in front of the other. In seeing Christ keep the Baillies, He showed Himself to be a sure foundation for my feet.

For we are his workmanship, created in Christ Jesus for good works, which God prepared beforehand, that we should walk in them.
Ephesians 2:10 ESV

Anna

—·—

CHAPTER 11

For God So Loved the World

For God so loved the world that He gave His only begotten Son, that whoever believes in Him should not perish but have everlasting life.

—

John 3:16 NKJV

A LESSON FOR THE JOURNEY

—·—

Today's pain is temporary; God's love is eternal.

"**H**ave you talked to the doctors lately about what it is going to be like when I die?" Gini asked. It was a very hard question to answer. A far easier question, and far more important one, was what would happen to my wife *after* she died. The answer to the second question was easy because God's promises never fail.

If you are a Christian, your life here on earth is merely a preparation for a far different life to come: the eternal life with Him that God promises to those whom He has called to Himself and have His Son in their hearts. As a mere mortal, your vision for the future is cloudy, like looking into a blurry mirror, but God's vision is perfect as He meets you where you are, whether in your study or in a hospital bed. His plans for you extend throughout all eternity. Yet to experience the joys of eternal life, you, like all of us, must first experience death.

In his book *A Grief Observed*, C. S. Lewis reflected on the death experience of his dear wife Joy. Lewis and his wife had been married only 3½ years, but Gini (*my joy!*) and I have been married for 49 glorious years. How richly we've been blessed!

As Gini and I think about our own lives, and our many years together as man and wife, we know that this is a time of turning to God in true thankfulness and rejoicing. We can rely completely upon Him and experience peace instead of anxious thoughts.

The fourth chapter of Philippians reminds us to re-joice "always." And since we are taught to rejoice at all times, we know that we must find reasons to rejoice, even during times of intense suffering or profound loss.

> *Rejoice in the Lord always; again I will say, rejoice. Let your reasonableness be known to everyone. The Lord is at hand; do not be anxious about anything, but in everything by prayer and supplication with thanks-giving let your requests be made known to God. And the peace of God, which surpasses all understanding, will guard your hearts and your minds in Christ Jesus. Finally, brothers, whatever is true, whatever is honor-able, whatever is just, whatever is pure, whatever is lovely, whatever is commendable, if there is any excel-lence, if there is anything worthy of praise, think about these things. What you have learned and received and heard and seen in me—practice these things, and the God of peace will be with you.*

Philippians 4:4-9 ESV

Today, would you take some time to think about death? Like Gini, would you consider the question, "What's it go-ing to be like when I die?"

More importantly, would you consider, for a moment, what it is going to be like *after* you die?

God's promise is that every tear will be wiped away, and all things will be made new. There will be no pain. No glioblastoma. We will see clearly the face of the One who formed us. We will be in the presence of the Almighty Creator of the universe and be known intimately by Him! With awe and amazement, ponder that for a moment! Heather, our youngest daughter, wrote me a note:

> I'm studying David and just read 2 Samuel 6-7. I saw David's emotions go from being angry to being afraid to being awed by God. I'm in the same situation as David, and I'm watching you go through some of those emotions too. Thank you for the reminder to be awed by our good God. Psalm 136:1 proclaims, "Oh, give thanks to the Lord, for He is good! For His mercy endures forever." That's the only final response we can have.

As you think about these things, please don't be afraid to discuss the particulars of your fears and beliefs with your loved ones.

You will spend eternity *either* in the presence of the Lord *or* separated from Him. And, even if you don't believe in eternity—even if you believe that death is the end and that nothing comes after it—please consider this: If you are wrong, you will have missed God's offer to accept His Son as Lord and Savior.

Gini and I both have the certain hope of eternal life with God. So, if you can understand the words on this page, I ask you to accept the Lord today. Please do not delay! Today, if you hear His voice, do not harden your hearts (Hebrews 3:15).

And we know that for those who love God
all things work together for good,
for those who are called according to his purpose.

—

Romans 8:28 ESV

LIGHT FOR OUR PATH FROM GOD'S WORD

So we do not lose heart. Though our outer self is wasting away, our inner self is being renewed day by day. For this light momentary affliction is preparing for us an eternal weight of glory beyond all comparison, as we look not to the things that are seen but to the things that are unseen. For the things that are seen are transient, but the things that are unseen are eternal.

2 Corinthians 4:16-18 ESV

And this is the will of Him who sent Me, that everyone who sees the Son and believes in Him may have everlasting life; and I will raise him up at the last day.

John 6:40 NKJV

And this is the testimony: that God has given us eternal life, and this life is in His Son. He who has the Son has life; he who does not have the Son of God does not have life.

1 John 5:11-12 NKJV

But as for you, O man of God, flee these things. Pursue righteousness, godliness, faith, love, steadfastness, gentleness. Fight the good fight of the faith. Take hold of the eternal life to which you were called and about which you made the good confession in the presence of many witnesses.

1 Timothy 6:11-12 ESV

MORE IMPORTANT IDEAS
ABOUT ETERNAL LIFE

Life is immortal, love eternal; death is nothing but a horizon, and a horizon is only the limit of our vision.

Corrie ten Boom

Teach us to set our hopes on heaven, to hold firmly to the promise of eternal life, so that we can withstand the struggles and storms of this world.

Max Lucado

I now know the power of the risen Lord! He lives! The dawn of Easter has broken in my own soul! My night is gone!

Mrs. Charles E. Cowman

Live near to God, and all things will appear little to you in comparison with eternal realities.

Robert Murray McCheyne

And because we know Christ is alive, we have hope for the present and hope for life beyond the grave.

Billy Graham

Christ is the only liberator whose liberation lasts forever.

Malcolm Muggeridge

GINI'S JOURNEY

A Tough Yet Joyous Conversation

In August of 2012, I posted the following message on CaringBridge.

Gini woke up this morning with a gleam in her eye and that pretty smile that many of you know. She is doing really well today with much better memory and good conversation. After a shower and breakfast, she decided we should sit in the sunroom to look out on the back yard with its trees and green. There was just that aura of joy and peace in her, and it flowed over to me as well.

After today's devotions about John 11 and Lazarus' death, Gini put her head back for what I thought would be a little rest and then said, "Have you talked to the doctors lately about what it is going to be like when I die?"

Then, we began a deep conversation about death. I told her that nothing had changed: the doctors thought that "if and when" the tumor returned, she would go into a coma and have a peaceful and pain-free death, as far as we can know. But, I told Gini that no one can be certain what she would feel or sense. I told her that during or as she went into a coma, she might continue to hear and understand things, but that she might not be able to talk or communicate. And, I promised that I would read comforting scriptures, hold her hand, and pray with her. I also reminded her that the Lord would be right there with her, holding her hand, too.

As we talked about death over the next days, I also read a few chapters from *O Love that Will Not Let Me Go*, a collection of sermons and writings edited by Nancy Guthrie. The authors in this book rely on the truth of God's Word and what it teaches about dying and heaven. In her forward, Guthrie likens each human life to a pregnancy where there is development and growth. And she compares heaven to the joyous experience of birth, and what lies beyond. But, she adds, to progress from pregnancy to birth, we must first go through labor and delivery!

It is often easier to talk about the life here and now, or about the great expectation of the heaven to come, but when we stop to think about the death experience, we are uncertain, and perhaps fearful of the unknown.

Gini went on to share that she was becoming a little impatient waiting for death. Initially, we had been told that, statistically, her life expectancy was between six months and two years. Then, as we experienced the joy of her continuing to live past six months with no tumor, followed by near death from blood clots, we came to another life-changing decision. We agreed that "we cannot both just sit here and wait to die!"

So, today, we are contemplating the things we can do with the time that the Lord has remaining for us on this earth. Our abilities and situation have changed, but the opportunities for ministry remain and our faithful Lord continues to guide and direct those opportunities into our path.

I cannot wait to see what the Lord continues to do with the rest of this day and the rest of our lives. The Lord is in charge of our days, and we continue to seek His will and purposes for each day He gives us life, breath, and all the things we need to carry out that will and purpose He has for us.

I assure you: Anyone who believes has eternal life.

—

John 6:47 HCSB

CHAPTER 12

—⁂—

Serve Him

*Now there are varieties of gifts, but the same Spirit.
And there are varieties of ministries, and the same Lord.*

—

1 Corinthians 12:4-5 NASB

A LESSON FOR THE JOURNEY

—⁂—

God isn't finished with you yet.
He still has important work for you to do,
and the time to begin that work is now.

I n Matthew 23:11, Jesus declares, "But he who is greatest among you shall be your servant" (NKJV). So, of this we can be sure: We achieve greatness, not through material wealth or earthly fame. We achieve greatness through service to others.

When we strive to be faithful servants of the Lord, He looks not only at the quality of our efforts, but also at the condition of our hearts. To serve Him generously, joyfully, and without complaint, is to follow in the footsteps of God's Son; it is an amazing journey filled with wonder and awe.

We are thankful that the Lord has given Gini, and all of us, the ability to go through this trial while finding new and different ways to honor Him. God has given us the power to endure and the strength to serve. And, we are truly thankful for prayers and encouragement that countless friends have offered to us. So many people have helped meet our needs physically and emotionally—in person and from a distance. We have been served by others even as we have tried, with God's help, to be faithful servants ourselves.

Today, this is my prayer for you. I pray that you will know, without any doubt, that the Lord isn't finished with you yet. To the contrary, He still has important tasks for you, tasks that are an integral part of His perfect plan. God will continue to bless the work of your hands as you serve

Him. And, if you are enduring difficult days, I pray that you will continue to be encouraged by the knowledge that the Lord allows us to experience hardships, trials, and suffering for our growth and maturity in Him *and* for His purposes and glory.

May we all continue to be bold servants as we proclaim how great God WAS, IS, and evermore WILL BE.

*Therefore, since we receive a kingdom which
cannot be shaken, let us show gratitude,
by which we may offer to God an acceptable service
with reverence and awe....*

—

Hebrews 12:28 NASB

LIGHT FOR OUR PATH FROM GOD'S WORD

For we are His workmanship, created in Christ Jesus for good works, which God prepared beforehand that we should walk in them.

Ephesians 2:10 NKJV

Suppose a brother or a sister is without clothes and daily food. If one of you says to him, "Go, I wish you well; keep warm and well fed," but does nothing about his physical needs, what good is it?

James 2:15-16 NIV

But a Samaritan, as he traveled, came where the man was; and when he saw him, he took pity on him. He went to him and bandaged his wounds, pouring on oil and wine. Then he put the man on his own donkey, took him to an inn and took care of him.

Luke 10:33-34 NIV

Be kindly affectionate to one another with brotherly love, in honor giving preference to one another; not lagging in diligence, fervent in spirit, serving the Lord; rejoicing in hope, patient in tribulation, continuing steadfastly in prayer.

Romans 12:10-12 NKJV

MORE IMPORTANT IDEAS ABOUT SERVING GOD

A servant of God has but one Master.

George Muller

If you aren't serving, you're just existing, because life is meant for ministry.

Rick Warren

You can judge how far you have risen in the scale of life by asking one question: How wisely and how deeply do I care? To be Christianized is to be sensitized. Christians are people who care.

E. Stanley Jones

You will find, as you look back upon your life, that the moments that stand out are the moments you have done things for others.

Henry Drummond

You have been used to take notice of the sayings of dying men. This is mine: that a life spent in the service of God, and communion with Him, is the most comfortable and pleasant life that anyone can live in this world.

Matthew Henry

GINI'S JOURNEY

Teaching His Word

Below is an excerpt from a birthday note that Gini received from one of her beloved mentees, a woman who also participated in Gini's inductive Bible study on the book of James. I think it expresses Gini's lifelong dedication to service as she continues to follow in the footsteps of her Lord *despite* the hardships she's endured.

Dear Gini,

When I think of you as my dear "Mother Gini," my heart is comforted and thankful. And, of course, I will always think of your smile! I imagine that there are only a handful of people that have a tremendous effect on each of us, and you are certainly one of those for me!

Here are a few highlights of the ways the Lord has used you in my life:

- † You taught me how to study His Word effectively.
- † You impressed upon me the value of hiding His Word in my heart.
- † You taught me to honor my husband in ways I had never fully appreciated.

† You seek to honor your husband, and you are always there for your girls and foster boys, even though they are grown.

† You are an example of "love in action," and you lay your life down for others.

† You offer constant hospitality.

† You offer encouragement that is always so specific.

† You are incredibly generous, and you "wear this world" loosely.

† You "keep things real" by letting others know that you, too, wrestle with sin.

† Your authenticity invites vulnerability. I know I am safe to reveal the real "me" to you.

† You lead a prayerful, spirit-filled life. I LOVE praying with you!

† You are full of wisdom. I have quoted you countless times.

† You are such good company. You're a joy to be around, and I laugh so much with you.

All these things show me that you are a vessel in the Master's hands. You are being used for a noble purpose, and I count it an honor to know you, and I thank God for your favor.

Love,
Bartges

May we all seek to serve the Lord in ways that bring Him glory and honor, ways that spur on and encourage our fellow travelers . . . and lead others to His throne. May we be the mothers and fathers and brothers and sisters God has called us to be. We're not home yet . . . so we're not done yet! Let us spend these precious days participating with our good and loving Father in His perfect plan, until we see Him face to face.

Whatever you do, do it enthusiastically,
as something done for the Lord and not for men.

—

Colossians 3:23 HCSB

— ✌ —

CHAPTER 13

You Are Protected

*Finally, my brethren, be strong in the Lord and
in the power of His might. Put on the whole armor
of God, that you may be able to stand against
the wiles of the devil.*

—

Ephesians 6:10-11 NKJV

A LESSON FOR THE JOURNEY

— ✌ —

God provides full armor for every
battle you'll ever face.

The world can be thought of as a battlefield, a place filled with more dangers and temptations than we can count. And, as long as we are on that battlefield, we are never secure *until* we put on the "full armor" of God. Perhaps you are envisioning a *Lord of the Rings* type battle, but our battles take place with our own testings, as real people living in a real world.

God has promised to protect us, and He intends to fulfill His promise. In a world filled with tragedy and trouble, God is our ultimate defense. In a world filled with misleading messages, God's Word is the ultimate truth. In a world where sickness and despair threaten us, God's never-ending love and provision is the answer to every temporary danger we face.

Today, I want to remind you that God is your greatest refuge and strength. When every earthly support system fails, God remains steadfast, and His love remains unchanged. When you encounter life's inevitable disappointments, God remains faithful. He is always with you, always ready to respond to your prayers according to His will and purposes, always working to turn temporary tragedy into eternal triumph.

It is no accident that this, the 13th chapter, carries within it an important message: to be wary of the natural human tendency to embrace superstitions, myths, and untruths of all kinds. Where there is untruth, there is also danger. So, we must prepare our hearts and minds for the struggles ahead. We must learn about God's armor: *how* it can be used, and *when* it should be used. And we must train ourselves, in advance of life's battles, so that we are "equipped" for the fight, even though we don't know when, where, or how long it will last. Read Psalm 3:3-4 about a complete, all-encompassing Shield who is also the Sustainer and lifter of our heads—before, in, and through a trial!

Recently, a young man called me and asked if he could stop by and talk with Gini and me. Of course, I said yes. After he arrived, the three of us spent time crying, talking, and sharing the Lord's counsel about the young man's continuing trial with alcohol. We told him that we could see the Lord's hand and protection in the trials that the young man now faced. And, he recognized that the time had come to stop trying to be in control; the time had come for him to turn everything over to the Lord, as there is no other way.

The young man was in his last semester of law school, but had spent several days of the previous week in a hospital detox unit where he was told that one more drop of alcohol might cause irreparable damage to his liver. So, he is taking his doctors' advice and taking a year off to be in a Christian rehabilitation facility, a place with no meds and a structured program to imprint a new lifestyle upon every facet of living. As the young man left our home, he asked Gini to "stay well" so he could see her more often in a year's time. Here are some texts that we exchanged after he left.

> **Gene**: "Mom and I just finished praying for u again. We are grateful that the Lord continues to use us in people's lives and especially in the lives of our children. We continue to be amazed at how His provision and your trust in Him has grown deeper and deeper through the years. Such as Mom emphasizing memorizing parts of Psalms and all of Philippians, and my giving you $s for memory verses. You said a couple times the verses came back to you and were very useful in times of trial and need. I see you trusting more in the Lord thru this and we both pray for conquering this so you will have the abundant and fruitful life u desire. Only He can do it in u but u have to trust and give up your control. Thanks for sharing and trusting us with this trial and allowing us to pray for you. Love you, but Jesus loves u more!"

> **Travis**: "Thank u so much, I'm not sure if I would ever have gotten to this place without the foundation that u guys have given me. I can't wait to see

how God wants to use me. And it was Ephesians 2:8-10 I was trying to remember: "For it is by grace you have been saved, through faith—and this is not from yourselves, it is the gift of God. Not by works, so that no man can boast. For we are God's workmanship, created in Christ Jesus to do good works, which God prepared in advance for us to do."

Gene: "You are loved and protected by the Lord! Trust Him and know He has provided the armor, allowed the testing, and will provide the way of escape from this bondage. 1 Corinthians 10:13 teaches us there is NO temptation or testing that is not common to all of us, God is faithful—He will not let u be tempted beyond your ability, and will provide the way of escape, that u will be enabled to endure it as well. Love, Dad"

As you now see, this young man is Travis, one of our foster sons; he lived with us for ten years. We love him, but Jesus loves him more. God is in the business of providing, protecting, preparing, and prevailing far in advance of the time and place of the battle!

On the next day, February 1st, Gini and I began our morning as we often do: by reading *Streams in the Desert*.

That day's devotional included the following excerpts, again just what God planned for us to be reading (and to be encouraged by) on the precise moment we needed it:

"This is my doing." (1 Kings 12:24) . . . only four words, but let them sink into your inner being, and use them as a pillow to rest your weary head . . . . I want you to learn when temptations attack you, and the enemy comes in "like a pent up flood" (Isaiah 59:19), that *"this is my doing"* and that your weakness needs My strength, and your safety lies in letting Me fight for you.... You did not come to this place by accident—you are exactly where I meant for you to be . . . .

"This is from Me," the Savior said, As bending low He kissed my brow, "For One who loves you thus has led. Just rest in Me, be patient now, Your Father knows you have need of this, Though, why perhaps you cannot see—Grieve not for things you've seemed to miss. The thing I send is best for thee." Then, looking through my tears, I plead, "Dear Lord, forgive, I did not know, It will not be hard since You do tread, Each path before me here below." And for my good this thing must be, His grace sufficient for

each test. So still I'll sing, "Whatever be God's way
for me is always best."

Trials come in all varieties, and most often they take us by surprise. We will pray for Travis, but we ask that you also pray for him and for others in the midst of similar lifelong battles.

Perhaps you are facing a life-threatening illness or a life-dominating sin. If so, my prayer for you is this: I pray that you will trust the Lord with a sincere heart and a focused mind. Don't be satisfied with a timid faith; ask God for the strength to endure the struggle, and continue to ask Him for that strength every day.

Will you accept God's strength today, and will you wear God's armor against the dangers of our world? When you do, you can live courageously, not in your own strength, efforts, or control; and know assuredly that you possess the ultimate protection: God's unfailing love for you.

LIGHT FOR OUR PATH FROM GOD'S WORD

Keep your life free from love of money, and be content with what you have, for he has said, "I will never leave you nor forsake you." So we can confidently say, "The Lord is my helper; I will not fear; what can man do to me?"

Hebrews 13:5-6 ESV

The Lord your God in your midst, The Mighty One, will save; He will rejoice over you with gladness, He will quiet you with His love, He will rejoice over you with singing.

Zephaniah 3:17 NKJV

Therefore take up the whole armor of God, that you may be able to withstand in the evil day, and having done all, to stand firm.

Ephesians 6:13 ESV

For by grace you have been saved through faith. And this is not your own doing; it is the gift of God, not a result of works, so that no one may boast. For we are his workmanship, created in Christ Jesus for good works, which God prepared beforehand, that we should walk in them.

Ephesians 2:8-10 ESV

What, then, shall we say in response to this? If God is for us, who can be against us?

Romans 8:31 NIV

For the Lord God is a sun and shield. The Lord gives grace and glory; He does not withhold the good from those who live with integrity. Lord of Hosts, happy is the person who trusts in You!

Psalm 84:11-12 HCSB

Unless the Lord guards the city, the watchman stays awake in vain.

Psalm 127:1b ESV

The Lord is my rock and my fortress and my deliverer, my God, my rock, in whom I take refuge, my shield, and the horn of my salvation, my stronghold.

Psalm 18:2 ESV

I will say of the LORD, He is my refuge and my fortress: my God, in him I will trust.

Psalm 91:2 KJV

MORE IMPORTANT IDEAS ABOUT
GOD'S PROTECTION

The disappointments of life are simply the hidden appointments of love.

C. A. Fox

The things that we mortals see as setbacks are, in truth, simply God's way of redirecting our paths toward Him. And what sometimes seems to be a terrible setback (to us) can always be transformed into a great victory (for Him). After all, no problem is too big for God.

Criswell Freeman (the man who helped me write this book)

Our future may look fearfully intimidating, yet we can look up to the Engineer of the Universe, confident that nothing escapes His attention or slips out of the control of those strong hands.

Elisabeth Elliot

A God wise enough to create me and the world I live in is wise enough to watch out for me.

Philip Yancey

We are never out of reach of Satan's devices, so we must never be without the whole armor of God.

Warren Wiersbe

I have a great need for Christ;
I have a great Christ for my need.

—

C. H. Spurgeon

GINI'S JOURNEY

Be Strong in the Lord

Because of Gini's illness, we have been made aware of many stories about families who are struggling faithfully against the deadly diagnosis of cancer. I received one such story from our daughter Heather. It is an amazing example of one family's immediate trust upon learning that their kindergarten boy had been diagnosed with leukemia.

Below is a note from the boy's father. I pray for you to have such a close relationship with God that, when (not if) each trial comes, you would have such trust; a trust that your family and others also immediately see; a trust that God provided for in advance:

Friends,

It has pleased the Lord, in His divine, providential, and Fatherly care, that a deep afflictive lot be cast to our family in this season of life, and I know, to you as well. If you are unaware, our 5-year-old son, Jett, was diagnosed with leukemia this past Wednesday.

This news has both shocked and shaken our souls with much sorrow and grief. Many tears have been shed as we struggle to digest the news, while at the same time effort to gird our hearts and bodies with all of the strength that the Lord works in us to minister to and care for his needs, both for the immediate battle and for the battle that lies ahead.

Nevertheless, we give thanks to our God and your God, through Jesus Christ, that this awful news has not shaken nor surprised our God and King. For, by God's abundant grace, we hold fast to the truth that He knows the end from the beginning (Isa. 46); He works all things, both the good and the bad, and from the smallest to the greatest, together for our eternal good, and his everlasting glory, and always according to the purpose of His will (Ephesians 1:11; Romans 8:28-33).

What a comfort we have from our God and Savior through Jesus Christ. For we do not long for, nor hope in the perishing, shifting, fading, indeed, dying things of this world; but we long for stability, life, goodness, and truth; in a word, we long for the Holy City of God (Hebrews 11), and cling to His promises, which are all YES and AMEN in Jesus Christ (2 Corinthians 1:20).

As we teach our children, we are constantly telling them that, "God is in charge, and He always does what is best (no matter what happens), and that there is nothing, either in heaven or on earth, that may escape his unsearchable and perfect purpose." Therefore, as we have been met with this affliction, we dare not change our verse or song, but rather, hold fast, through our and your prayers, as well as God's grace and promises that these things hold both true and fast no matter what happens; for, the King truly has no shadow.

I speak of these things above, not with great strength, but rather, with fearful and trembling hope. For, our child has cancer, and cancer's desire is to kill, regardless of the statistics. Nevertheless, this hope, as God has ordered it, we receive through your prayers, which rise as bowls of incense to our God with great pleasure. "God is there," as Francis Schaffer said, "He is there, and He is awaiting the broken cries of the saints."

We know and trust that God has brought us here both to minister and to be ministered to. What a joy and encouragement it is to have you, and for us to be had and held by our Lord Jesus Christ.

> Grace and Peace be multiplied to you,
> *Jes, a prayerful father in Texas*

Only through training your mind and heart by Bible study and prayer can you be prepared and know how to put on, and to take up, the full armor. Then, you can be strong in the Lord.

Gini's and my prayer for you is that you prepare to put on, and prepare to take up, God's armor as is taught to us in Ephesians 6:10-18:

Finally, be strong in the Lord and in the strength of his might. Put on the whole armor of God, that you may be able to stand against the schemes of the devil. For we do not wrestle against flesh and blood, but against the rulers, against the authorities, against the cosmic powers over this present darkness, against the spiritual forces of evil in the heavenly places. Therefore take up the whole armor of God, that you may be able to withstand in the evil day, and having done all, to stand firm. Stand therefore, having fastened on the belt of truth, and having put on the breastplate of righteousness, and, as shoes for your feet, having put on the readiness given by the gospel of peace. In all circumstances take up the shield of faith, with which you can extinguish all the flaming darts of the evil one; and take the helmet of salvation, and the sword of the Spirit, which is the word of God, praying at all times in

*the Spirit, with all prayer and supplication. To that end
keep alert with all perseverance, making supplication
for all the saints.*

Our grandchildren have these verses in their minds
and hearts, through singing them. With God's help, may
they continue to prepare themselves for their trials, being
strong in the Lord and in the strength of His might.

We have a God who delights in impossibilities.

—

Andrew Murray

CHAPTER 14

—∞—

Infinite Blessings

I will lift up my eyes to the mountains;
from whence shall my help come?
My help comes from the Lord,
who made the heaven and earth.

—

Psalm 121:1-2 NASB

A LESSON FOR THE JOURNEY

—∞—

In every stage of your journey,
through happy times and trying times,
you are blessed beyond measure.

"Count your many blessings, name them one by one . . . " If you sat down and began counting your blessings, how long would it take? A very, very long time! Your blessings include life, freedom, family, friends, talents, and possessions, for starters. But, your greatest blessing is God's gift of salvation through Christ Jesus. Is the Lord calling you to Himself? Is He calling you to change the way you have been living? Is He asking you to just stop and be quiet before Him? Listen to this passage from 2 Corinthians 6 "In the time of My favor I heard you, and in the day of salvation I helped you. I tell you, now is the time of God's favor, now is the day of salvation" (v. 2).

Gini and I often reflect on the blessings we've received on our journey so far. And, as we near the end of our lives on this earth, we know what a privilege it is to pass on the banner of the Lord to our children, to their children, to *all* our family members (far beyond the biological), to our friends, and even to strangers. I again repeat Gini's life verse, 3 John 4: "I have no greater joy than to hear my children [including *all* our family] are walking in the truth."

Gini and I believe that we honor God, in part, by the genuine gratitude we feel in our hearts for the blessings He has bestowed upon us. Yet sometimes, we must travel through periods of anxiety and fear. On life's darker days, we seek to cleanse our hearts, as best we can, of negative emotions. We seek to fill our hearts, instead, with praise, with love, with hope, and with thanksgiving.

And don't forget that what we may consider a loss or disadvantage is really a blessing. Here's an example. One of our daughters has some short-term memory loss because of encephalitis as an adult. She can no longer be a nurse because she might not remember to give a pill, or she might forget when a particular medication had been given to a patient. But, both her husband and I consider it a blessing because we both remember things too well! We both have difficulty forgetting, and thus have more trouble forgiving. The Bible tells us the Lord forgives our sin and remembers it no more; in fact, our sin is removed as far as the east is from the west!

Today, I challenge you to begin thinking seriously about *your own* blessings. Even if you can name only a small percentage of the gifts God has given you, I can assure you that your list will be a long one. Although you most certainly will not be able to make a complete list of God's gifts, I urge you to take a few moments and jot down as many blessings as you can. Then, give thanks to the Giver of all good things: God. Based on God's promise to Abraham in Genesis 12:2-3 and applying it to our lives, I believe God has showered each of us with blessings that we might be watered and grow; but not only that we might be blessed, but also that we would be a blessing to all we interact with.

The Lord's love for you is eternal, as are His blessings. And it's never too soon—or too late—to offer Him thanks. Accept His greatest Gift as a blessing—*and to be a blessing.*

Bless the Lord, O my soul,
and forget not all His benefits.

—

Psalm 103:2 NKJV

LIGHT FOR OUR PATH FROM GOD'S WORD

I will make you into a great nation, and I will bless you; I will make your name great, and you will be a blessing, I will bless those who bless you, and whoever curses you I will curse; and all peoples on earth will be blessed through you.

Genesis 12:2-3 NIV

I, even I, am the one who wipes out your transgressions for My own sake, and I will not remember your sins.

Isaiah 43:25 NASB

As far as the east is from the west, so far has He removed our transgressions from us.

Psalm 103:12 NKJV

Blessed be the Lord, who daily bears our burden, the God who is our salvation.

Psalm 68:19 NASB

Blessed be the Lord, who daily loads us with benefits, the God of our salvation!

Psalm 68:19 NKJV

God is our refuge and strength, a very present help in trouble.

Psalm 46:1 KJV

MORE IMPORTANT IDEAS ABOUT
GOD'S BLESSINGS

We prevent God from giving us the great spiritual gifts He has in store for us, because we do not give thanks for daily gifts.

Dietrich Bonhoeffer

God wants his people to earnestly seek his will and to pray for it, and thus to become agents of the blessing God brings.

James Montgomery Boice

Grace comes from the heart of a gracious God who wants to stun you and overwhelm you with a gift you don't deserve—salvation, adoption, a spiritual ability to use in kingdom service, answered prayer, the church, His presence, His wisdom, His guidance, His love.

Bill Hybels

Prayer is the way and means God has appointed for the communication of the blessings of His goodness to His people.

A. W. Pink

Temptation may even be a blessing to a man when it reveals to him his weakness and drives him to the almighty Savior. Do not be surprised, then, dear child of God, if you are tempted at every step of your earthly journey, and almost beyond endurance.

F. B. Myer

Blessings can either humble us and draw us closer to God or allow us to become full of pride and self-sufficiency.

Jim Cymbala

God is more anxious to bestow His blessings on us than we are to receive them.

St. Augustine

Romans is really the chief part of the New Testament, and is truly the purest gospel. It is not only that every Christian should know it word for word, by heart, but also that he should occupy himself with it every day, as the daily bread of the soul. We can never read it or ponder over it too much, for the more we deal with it, the more precious it becomes and the better it tastes.

Martin Luther

GINI'S JOURNEY

Invest in People

When we first moved to Anderson, South Carolina, Gini met Elsie. They studied the Bible together, taught one another, taught their children, and encouraged their husbands to do the same. Then, they taught others separately and together in numerous inductive Bible studies.

While teaching, Gini always encouraged memorization of large passages of God's Word, and used accountability aids. One mentee, Ann-Janette even studied together with Gini using weekly hour-long calls (made by Gini) from Australia!

Ann-Janette and another woman, Rona, had previously arranged to say their entire passages to Gini on the day after her surgery. Ann-Janette and Rona thought they might have some "extra time," but Gini remembered their appointment and had them come to the hospital on the fourth day after surgery! Through tears, Ann-Janette recited all of Romans 8, and Rona recited all of Colossians 3, while Gini gently "corrected" a few words, from her bed, and without a Bible in hand.

Below is an excerpt from a message that was sent to Gini from Rona. As you can see, Rona was blessed by Gini's Bible-study group and by Gini's emphasis on memorization. I'm certain that Rona will, in turn, impart those blessings to others.

Dear Gini,

When I think of the ways you've influenced my life, one thing comes to the forefront above all others, and that is your love for God's Word. I have been a Christian for a long time, went to a Bible college, was a missionary, was in a great teaching church for many years, and have several friends who have been spiritual mentors to me. But, I can honestly say I have been affected and influenced by you, more than anyone else in my life, to love God's Word, to study it, and to memorize it.

I joined your James Bible study and haven't been the same since. I learned so much. Thanks for helping me add to my "Bible study tool bag." Learning how to inductively study the Bible has been such an important part of my spiritual growth in the last few years, and it has caused my love for His Word to grow exponentially. Beyond that, your challenge to memorize the Word has been life-changing.

I had memorized verses here and there, and many of them had stuck in my brain, but when you first suggested memorizing ALL of the first chapter of James, I thought, "She's crazy! There is no way I can do that!" It really didn't seem possible to me. But thanks to your perseverance and gentle encouragement, I decided to give it a try. I was (and continue to be) blessed beyond measure.

Thank you, Gini, for investing in me! It will have lasting dividends not only for me, but by God's grace, also for my children and the other women God places in my life. Thank you for being a godly example and living life in front of me in a way that causes me to glorify Him for the way He works. I so appreciate you and your love for our Savior, and I love you and Gene so much.

Love you,
Rona

Today, Gini and I pray that you will go forth and be a blessing, investing your every thought, word, and deed!

CHAPTER 15

The Storms Are Part of His Plan

Blessed is a man who endures trials, because
when he passes the test he will receive the crown of life
that He has promised to those who love Him.

—

James 1:12 HCSB

A LESSON FOR THE JOURNEY

The inevitable, and temporary, storms of life
are a part of God's eternal plan. Even though
you cannot fully understand His plan,
you must always trust the Planner.

As we grow in God-given holiness, it is not without suffering. In fact, God uses the very trials we dread as tools to mold us into the creatures He intends for us to become, to make us know how much we are dependent upon Him, and to know "that it's all about God," and *not* about ourselves. Along the way, He does help us to pass the test of the trials we endure.

The inevitability of death, like the sting of affliction, helps us concentrate our thoughts on the things that are *really* important. As the end draws nearer, the real meaning of life becomes clearer as we stop valuing the things of this world and stop pursuing foolish ideas. Instead, we aim our gaze more and more on God.

With the mention of aim—as I sit here writing, above my desk is a handcrafted arrow. It was given to me several years ago by my young elder friend Dale when I mentioned that we need to be "straight arrows" for the Lord. It hangs along with a note including Isaiah 49:2 about how the Lord made our mouth a sharpened sword hidden in His hand, and a polished arrow concealed in His quiver. So, let me tell you a short story about arrow-making.

First, select a proper limb and remove it from the tree, then allow it to dry under very controlled conditions. Next, remove the bark and whittle down the wood to the right diameter, avoiding knots and other defects—all the time checking to make sure the arrow is straight and true.

Then, sand the surface and apply a coating or polish it smooth. And finally, carefully put the proper feathers and notch at one end, and the arrowhead at the other.

We want to be straight arrows for the Lord, useful for His intended purpose. He has torn off our bark, whittled, sanded, and polished us, then put us in His quiver, to be aimed and used by Him—arrows in the hand of a loving God! We will be shot into battle. God's aim is straight and true; each of us will land at the precise target spot and for the purpose He intends.

For Gini and me, our primary focus is now on God's purpose for our remaining days here on this earth. We want to allow the Lord to use us as He pleases, as arrows for His glory. Our emotions are being weaned away from life's everyday distractions. We can now let circumstances be what they may as we continue to seek only God and His will, with a calm assurance that He is causing *every-thing*, whether pleasant or troubling, to work for the good of those who love Him. Now that the end of life has become so real to us, our reasoning has become calm and quiet because so many "dead-end" options have been removed.

Truly, the things of earth are growing strangely dim in the light of His marvelous grace. And, as we think about our journey destination and any legacy left behind, we know that our children and grandchildren are also being molded into such arrows. Thus, a part of our journey has been, and continues to be, encouraging and spurring them on as they are taught, corrected, and trained. Their starting point was somewhere around the midpoint of our journey, and their earthly end point will likely be beyond ours.

The concluding chapters of Ecclesiastes have much to teach us about storms. The eleventh chapter begins with these familiar words: "Cast your bread upon the waters, for you will find it after many days. Give a portion to seven, or even to eight, for you know not what disaster may happen on earth. If the clouds are full of rain, they empty themselves on the earth, and if a tree falls to the south or to the north, in the place where the tree falls, there it will lie."

We all know the old adage "April showers bring May flowers." And, another saying, similar but less familiar, is "It's raining flowers." Both these aphorisms remind us that the earth needs rain, and that beautiful things inevitably grow, even after the tempest. How comforting it is to know that the same clouds that bring the deluge also provide the waters that cause seeds to grow and flowers to blossom. Many quotes tell of blessings followed by battles; there are also the trials that are followed by blessings!

I received this note from my middle daughter, Kim:

Dear Dad,

I just want you to know how incredibly proud I am of you for loving Mom so well in her illness and for "leaning into" what God has for you and not running from it. I doubt I will ever receive a present as sweetly given as you giving me one of Mom's hummingbird mugs. As I pray, I think of you both happily every morning with my coffee.

I love you Dad,
Kim

God has a purpose and a plan for the storms of life; it is a plan to mature us and to produce the fruit He desires. By *letting go* and *letting God* continue to mold us and hold our hand, we will finish well by purposing to finish well. In the midst of our "stormy" days, the Lord continues to provide opportunities for us to witness. Nearly every time either I, or both Gini and I, go to the grocery store or a restaurant, we meet someone who wants to see us, or someone who wants to encourage us, or someone who asks us to pray for them. These encounters are sometimes timed by the Lord down to the exact second, as we could disappear down a grocery aisle and never be seen. In fact, in one instance at an interstate rest stop, I was spotted just getting into our car when a friend's car was pulling into the rest area! God is amazing in His plan and in His detailed ordering of the circumstances.

Psalm 29 teaches us about the "Perfect Storm": "Ascribe to the Lord glory and strength. Ascribe to the Lord the glory due his name; worship the Lord in the splendor of holiness. The voice of the Lord is over the waters . . ." (vv. 1-3, ESV).

The Psalmist instructs us to hear the Lord's voice over the waters and through the thunder and fire. So, the next time you see dark clouds forming upon *your* horizon, wait upon the Lord and trust His plan. He is a loving, Sovereign God. And, He uses both the sun *and* the rain (and even the fiercest damaging storm) to bring forth His eternal harvest.

He knows when we go into the storm,
He watches over us in the storm,
and He can bring us out of the storm when
His purposes have been fulfilled.

—

Warren Wiersbe

LIGHT FOR OUR PATH FROM GOD'S WORD

Blessed be the God and Father of our Lord Jesus Christ, who has blessed us in Christ with every spiritual blessing in the heavenly places, even as he chose us in him before the foundation of the world, that we should be holy and blameless before him. In love he predestined us for adoption as sons through Jesus Christ, according to the purpose of his will, to the praise of his glorious grace, with which he has blessed us in the Beloved. In him we have redemption through his blood, the forgiveness of our trespasses, according to the riches of his grace, which he lavished upon us, in all wisdom and insight.

Ephesians 1:3-8 ESV

Be strong and courageous. Do not be terrified; do not be discouraged, for the LORD your God will be with you wherever you go.

Joshua 1:9 NIV

My grace is sufficient for you, for my power is made perfect in weakness.

2 Corinthians 12:9 NIV

Wait on the LORD: be of good courage, and he shall strengthen thine heart: wait, I say, on the LORD.

Psalm 27:14 KJV

151

Sow for yourselves righteousness; reap steadfast love; break up your fallow ground, for it is the time to seek the Lord, that he may come and rain righteousness upon you.

Hosea 10:12 ESV

And what you have heard from me in the presence of many witnesses, commit to faithful men who will be able to teach others also. Share in suffering as a good soldier of Christ Jesus.

2 Timothy 2:2-3 HCSB

Like arrows in the hands of a warrior are children born in one's youth. Blessed is the man whose quiver is full of them.

Psalm 127:4-5a ESV

He made my mouth like a sharpened sword, in the shadow of his hand he hid me; he made me into a polished (or select) arrow and concealed me in his quiver.

Isaiah 49:2 NIV

The Lord sits enthroned over the flood; the Lord sits enthroned as king forever. May the Lord give strength to his people! May the Lord bless his people with peace!

Psalm 29:10-11 ESV

MORE IMPORTANT IDEAS ABOUT GOD'S PLAN THROUGH ADVERSITY

What a comfort to know that God is present there in your life, available to meet every situation with you, that you are never left to face any problem alone.

Vonette Bright

Suffering will be either your master or your servant, depending on how you handle the crises of life.

Warren Wiersbe

Through all of the crises of life—and we all are going to experience them—we have this magnificent Anchor.

Franklin Graham

The born-again Christian sees life not as a blurred, confused, meaningless mass, but as something planned and purposeful.

Billy Graham

God has a course mapped out for your life, and all the inadequacies in the world will not change His mind. He will be with you every step of the way. And though it may take time, He has a celebration planned for when you cross over the "Red Seas" of your life.

Charles Swindoll

GINI'S JOURNEY

His Perfect, Mysterious Ways

Below are the words from one of Gini's favorite hymns. It's one of my favorites, too, because it reminds me that the Lord "works His sovereign will" for a purpose that is unknowable to me but completely understood by Him.

How comforting it is to know that the very clouds we fear are, in truth, "big with mercy" and that they yield so many blessings!

GOD MOVES IN MYSTERIOUS WAYS
By William Cowper

God moves in a mysterious way,
His wonders to perform;
He plants his footsteps in the sea,
And rides upon the storm.
Deep in unfathomable mines
Of never failing skill,
He treasures up his bright designs,
And works his sovereign will.
Ye fearful saints, fresh courage take,
The clouds ye so much dread
are big with mercy, and shall break

In blessings on your head.
Judge not the Lord by feeble sense,
But trust him for his grace;
Behind a frowning providence,
He hides a smiling face.
His purposes will ripen fast,
Unfolding every hour;
The bud may have a bitter taste,
But sweet will be the flower.
Blind unbelief is sure to err,
And scan his work in vain;
God is his own interpreter,
And he will make it plain.

I'll conclude with a message from my dear wife:

There truly is a cycle in our lives that includes blessings followed by times of trial and testing. It is God's way of maturing us and preparing us for the trials to come. But, after each battle, we are again blessed if we can see the blessing of the trial. We see how God has not only matured us, but also used us.

Through this trial of ours, both Gene and I have become the arrows in His hands that He is lovingly preparing for the next battle. And we are rejoicing that we can count on Him to mysteriously perform His wonders yet again. One such wonder is helping and seeing God help Gene write these words, as his writing skills needed honing, whittling, and polishing for sure!

Love,
Gini

I will bless them and the places surrounding my hill.
I will send down showers in season;
there will be showers of blessings.

—

Ezekiel 34:26 NIV

CHAPTER 16

—⁓—

He Gives Strength

*And He said to me, "My grace is sufficient for you,
for My strength is made perfect in weakness."*

—

2 Corinthians 12:9 NKJV

A LESSON FOR THE JOURNEY

—⁓—

When you're too tired—or too afraid—to take
another step, God can give you the strength
and courage you need.

Gini trusted and knew she had the strength to "get over" her initial surgery. The operation was, for her, like a mountain she would climb with God's help. But, after surgery, chemotherapy, and several serious setbacks, Gini came to the realize that this first mountain—surgery—was only the beginning. She could see that more peaks and valleys lay ahead.

Fighting cancer, or any other serious illness—or simply battling the inevitable ravages of the aging process—is not like climbing a single mountain; it's like climbing an entire range! When we reach the peak, the rest is often short and we discover a dark valley or river to cross on the other side that gives way to yet another, perhaps steeper climb.

Where can we find the strength to climb, not one mountain, but many? And where can we summon the courage to endure the dark valleys or deep rivers in between? I know of no source other than God.

Below is a CaringBridge post about the 23rd Psalm. I wrote it on July 15, 2011, just five days before Gini developed devastating blood clots to her lungs that brought her to the brink of death. And, one week later, she was found to have bone marrow failure with insufficient red cells and platelets in her blood. Although Gini *did* walk through the valley of the shadow of death during these agonizing days, and although we were both shaken to the core by these relapses, we knew she was protected by our loving Heavenly Father because we have seen the Lord's faithfulness time and again as we have rested and trusted in Him.

VALLEYS AND RIVERS TO CROSS!

Psalm 23 is one we all know so well, and it applies to Gini and my life in many ways this last couple weeks. We have gone through the valleys with the Lord holding our hands and guiding each step with the sure promise of His goodness and mercy; and that we indeed shall dwell in His house forever.

Gini still has extreme tiredness accompanied by weakness which sometimes causes her to just collapse in mid- step, so we have to help assist with most everything. But we see joyful moments of the Lord's strength. And, we see His hand pulling her through.

The LORD is my shepherd; I shall not want. He makes me lie down in green pastures. He leads me beside still waters. He restores my soul. He leads me in paths of righteousness for his name's sake. Even though I walk through the valley of the shadow of death, I will fear no evil, For you are with me; your rod and your staff, they comfort me. You prepare a table before me in the presence of my enemies; You anoint my head with oil; my cup overflows. Surely goodness and mercy shall follow me all the days of my life, and I shall dwell in the house of the LORD forever.

The 23rd Psalm reminds us that God is our Shepherd, always watching over us. When we are weary, He offers strength. When we see no hope, God reminds us of His promises. When we grieve, He wipes away our tears.

Do you feel overwhelmed by today's challenges? Are you feeling the toil of a body wearing out or seeing a loved one deteriorate? Are you weary from your own journey that is sapping your strength? Are you emotionally drained and in a deep valley, a caretaker needing rest? Do you feel stung by physical or emotional pain? Are you in the darkest part of the valley, or in the deepest water, feeling overwhelmed by the struggles of today and the fears of tomorrow? Turn your concerns and your prayers over to God. He knows your needs, and He has promised to meet those needs. Whatever your circumstances, the Lord will protect you and care for you. Invite Him into your heart and allow Him to renew your spirit. He will never fail you. Look up as unto the hills for the Lord's strength and courage to take the next steps on the path of your journey.

LIGHT FOR OUR PATH FROM GOD'S WORD

Do you not know? Have you not heard? The Everlasting God, the LORD, the Creator of the ends of the earth does not become weary or tired. His understanding is inscrutable. He gives strength to the weary, and to him who lacks might He increases power. Though youths grow weary and tired, and vigorous young men stumble badly, yet those who wait for the LORD will gain new strength; they will mount up with wings like eagles, they will run and not get tired, they will walk and not become weary.

Isaiah 40:28-31 NASB

Be strong! We must prove ourselves strong for our people and for the cities of our God. May the Lord's will be done.

1 Chronicles 19:13 HCSB

I will lift up my eyes to the hills—from whence comes my help? My help comes from the Lord, who made heaven and earth.

Psalm 121:1-2 NKJV

Cast your burden on the Lord, and He shall sustain you; He shall never permit the righteous to be moved.

Psalm 55:22 NKJV

MORE IMPORTANT IDEAS ABOUT FINDING STRENGTH

He giveth more grace as our burdens grow greater, / He sendeth more strength as our labors increase; / To added afflictions He addeth His mercy, / To multiplied trials He multiplies peace.

Annie Johnson Flint

Cast yourself into the arms of God and be very sure that if He wants anything of you, He will fit you for the work and give you strength.

Philip Neri

In leaning upon His Cross, let me not refuse my own; yet in bearing mine, let me bear it by the strength of His.

John Baillie (my namesake Scottish theologian)

God gives us always strength enough, and sense enough, for everything He wants us to do.

John Ruskin

Courage means being the man God created you to be— in the moments He created for you to be that man— regardless of the obstacles, whether enemies external or doubts internal, regardless of the cost.

Dale Treash

GINI'S JOURNEY

A Phone Call to Remember

Gini's friend Carol lived in our hometown of Anderson, South Carolina, before moving to Arizona. When she and her husband, Jim, moved away, Jim was a non-Christian who hardly ever set foot inside a church but would come to church social functions, including some at our home.

When Gini said goodbye to Jim, she told him that the Lord was calling him to Arizona. Gini added that *when* (not *if*) he accepted the Lord, Jim should call her.

After several months had passed, I was at home one day, and the phone rang. I answered, and it was Jim; he asked to speak with Gini.

Gini and I both began to weep as I handed her the phone with, "It's Jim," because we knew what he was going to say. And we were right: Jim had accepted Jesus!

Below is a birthday note Carol later sent to Gini:

Dear Gini,

I'm just thinking of you and one of my favorite memories of you is of your sitting at the piano at church and smiling at me. I will always remember how you were an accomplished pianist, but took additional lessons just so you could serve Christ in that way.

You and Gene took the time to love on our family and for this we thank Jesus for putting you in our lives. I thank God that He sent us to Anderson, so that we could meet you and Gene, and then Jim could meet Jesus.

I pray that you have a most special and blessed birthday. May you know that you are loved, for you shine so brightly for Jesus, who could not love you?

Love and prayers,
Carol

It takes faith to sense the Lord working in someone, and it takes courage to tell—or even challenge—that person by sharing what you are sensing that the Lord is doing in his or her life. Again, you see how Gini followed the Lord's leading with heart and voice. I, too, often sit and watch the Lord at work. How I need my wife's God-given boldness more often.

CHAPTER 17

Beyond All the Worries

*But seek first the kingdom of God and His
righteousness, and all these things shall be added to you.
Therefore do not worry about tomorrow,
for tomorrow will worry about its own things.
Sufficient for the day is its own trouble.*

—

Matthew 6:33-34 NKJV

A LESSON FOR THE JOURNEY

God wants you to take your worries to Him,
and to leave them there.

I f you or a loved one is battling a serious illness, I don't have to tell you what it means to lie awake at night and worry about all the things you *can't* control. You've probably had enough of those nights already; in fact, you could probably write *your own* book about the anguish of anxiety.

Gini and I have experienced our own sleepless nights, too, struggling to deal with the realities of cancer and the inevitabilities of death. We've cried together and worried together on many occasions, but afterwards, we have always tried to turn our fears into prayers. And, in our better moments, when we have quietly turned our thoughts and hearts over to the Lord, He comforted us in ways that no one on earth could. When every other support system proved insufficient, the Lord provided the assurance and the peace we needed at *precisely* the moment we needed it. In short, God kept the promise of Philippians 4:7; He guarded our hearts. And, because we've trusted the Lord completely, we've avoided a two-fold temptation: the temptation to second-guess ourselves *and* to second-guess our Lord's perfect plan for us.

Because you have the ability to think, you were born with all the intellectual equipment you'll ever need to become a world-class worrier. In fact, your amazing brain can manufacture more doubts and fears than you can count. If you allow those thoughts to run wild, you catch yourself imagining an endless array of unfavorable outcomes, most of which will never happen.

Jesus understood your concerns when He spoke the reassuring words found in the 6th chapter of Matthew:

> *Therefore I say to you, do not worry about your life, what you will eat or what you will drink; nor about your body, what you will put on. Is not life more than food and the body more than clothing? Look at the birds of the air, for they neither sow nor reap nor gather into barns; yet your heavenly Father feeds them. Are you not of more value than they? Which of you by worrying can add one cubit to his stature? . . . Therefore do not worry about tomorrow, for tomorrow will worry about its own things. Sufficient for the day is its own trouble* (vv. 25-27, 34 NKJV)

Today I ask you to take just the next step and not even start down any "what if" rabbit trails. Take your worries to God; take your troubles to Him; take your fears to Him; take your doubts to Him; take your weaknesses to Him; take your sorrows to Him . . . and leave them all there. Build your spiritual house upon the Rock that cannot be moved.

Of course, it is easy to talk about building on the Rock, or singing about, "Leaving it all with Jesus." But, how, exactly, can you cast everything on the Lord? I can think of three specifics to get you started. First, set your mind on things above; second, take every thought captive; and third, call to mind how the Lord has shown you His previous faithfulness.

Twenty-one months after Gini's initial diagnosis, we returned to the Duke Medical Center for a regular follow-up visit. Although we had expected the best, the news was not at all what we wanted to hear: the MRI revealed the possibility that the tumor had returned.

After discussing the MRI and answering our immediate questions, Dr. Katy Peters and the medical team left the room. Gini and I looked at one another, and I prayed with her. Then, I repeated the same words I had spoken when we first found out about her cancer almost two years before. I said, "This is the day the Lord has made, let us rejoice and be glad in it."

Gini replied, "In everything give thanks for this is the will of God in Christ Jesus concerning you."

Truly, the Lord does give us a choice *not* to rejoice, but Gini and I have chosen to have our joy and strength in the Lord and to rest in Him, taking one step at a time.

LIGHT FOR OUR PATH FROM GOD'S WORD

But this I call to mind, and therefore I have hope: The steadfast love of the Lord never ceases; his mercies never come to an end; they are new every morning; great is your faithfulness. "The Lord is my portion," says my soul, "therefore I will hope in him."

Lamentations 3:21-24 ESV

Humble yourselves, therefore, under the mighty hand of God so that at the proper time he may exalt you, casting all your anxieties on him, because he cares for you. Be sober-minded; be watchful. Your adversary the devil prowls around like a roaring lion, seeking someone to devour. Resist him, firm in your faith, knowing that the same kinds of suffering are being experienced by your brotherhood throughout the world. And after you have suffered a little while, the God of all grace, who has called you to his eternal glory in Christ, will himself restore, confirm, strengthen, and establish you. To him be the dominion forever and ever.

1 Peter 5:6-11 ESV

Be anxious for nothing, but in everything by prayer and supplication with thanksgiving let your requests be made known to God.

Philippians 4:6 NASB

MORE IMPORTANT IDEAS ABOUT OVERCOMING WORRY

Anxiety does not empty tomorrow of its sorrows, but only empties today of its strength.

C. H. Spurgeon

We are not called to be burden-bearers, but cross-bearers and light-bearers. We must cast our burdens on the Lord.

Corrie ten Boom

This life of faith, then, consists in just this—being a child in the Father's house. Let the ways of childish confidence and freedom from care, which so please you and win your heart when you observe your own little ones, teach you what you should be in your attitude toward God.

Hannah Whitall Smith

Live near to God, and all things will appear little to you in comparison with eternal realities.

Robert Murray McCheyne

Are you tired of chasing pretty rainbows? Are you tired of spinning round and round? Wrap up all those shattered dreams of your life and at the feet of Jesus, lay them down.

Phil Johnson

GINI'S JOURNEY

He Is Able to Guard

The Lord tells us not to be fearful because He has great promises for our future. He can see the glorious place He has prepared for us, and all He asks is that we trust Him until the day He calls us home.

Immediately after her brain surgery, Gini was very confused, and those of us who loved her were understandably concerned. From time to time, my own legitimate concerns turned toward anxious and fretful worry. That's when I slowed myself down long enough to catch my breath and talk to God.

I prayed that Gini's confusion would pass and, for the most part, it did. As I think back on those discouraging days, I reflect on the encouraging words from 2 Timothy 1:6-14:

For this reason I remind you to fan into flame the gift of God, which is in you through the laying on of my hands, for God gave us a spirit not of fear but of power and love and self-control. Therefore do not be ashamed of the testimony about our Lord, nor of me his prisoner, but share in suffering for the gospel by the power of God, who saved us and called us to a holy calling, not because of our works but because of his own purpose and grace, which he gave us in Christ Jesus before the ages began, and which now has been manifested through the appearing of our Savior Christ Jesus, who abolished death and brought life and immortality to light through the gospel, for which I was appointed a preacher and apostle and teacher, which is why I suffer as I do. But I am not ashamed, for I know whom I have believed, and I am convinced that he is able to guard until that Day what has been entrusted to me. Follow the pattern of the sound words that you have heard from me, in the faith and love that are in Christ Jesus. By the Holy Spirit who dwells within us, guard the good deposit entrusted to you.

Perhaps you are concerned about your own or a loved one's health and future. Or, perhaps you are simply a "worrier" by nature. If so, Gini and I pray that you will remember this: He is able to guard your heart and mind. Your precious Lord still sits in His heaven and you are His beloved child. He wants to comfort you and lead you home. Sing the song from the above scripture, "I know whom I have believed . . ." So, please worry a little less and trust God a little more because God is trustworthy . . . and you can lean on His everlasting arms.

CHAPTER 18

—❧—

You Can Help

Carry one another's burdens;
in this way you will fulfill the law of Christ.

—

Galatians 6:2 HCSB

A LESSON FOR THE JOURNEY

—❧—

As you travel through life, God will give you
countless opportunities to serve Him by serving
His children. Be watchful for these opportunities
and seize them while you journey.

Two months after her surgery, Gini seemed to be having one hard day after another. Radiation treatments left her weak; she had trouble communicating her thoughts, and she was understandably irritated much of the time.

When I related these problems to one of "our" doctors, he responded without hesitation. The doctor said, "Gene, I can help with this."

I expected the physician to recommend some easy medical solution, or perhaps a different medication. Instead, he gave me terrific piece of advice; he said, "She can't help it, but you can."

I said nothing, so the doctor repeated himself: "Gene, did you hear me? Gini *can't* help it, but *you* can."

I realized that his advice was, essentially, the same advice I have gotten (and given) over the years: We can't control the other person, but we can control ourselves. And that's a message worth remembering when we're caring for loved ones who sometimes cannot *think* or *care* for themselves. Sometimes it is gentle words, sometimes helping to lift, sometimes a helping hand, sometimes just holding hands. Thankfully, we have many chances to just hold one another's hands.

Years ago, a young man asked me to study the Bible with him before he got married. In the process, he picked my brain for marital advice. I told him that my best advice was simply this: he would have to "die to self."

After the young man had been married a few years, we talked again, and he said that he *really* appreciated my advice about "dying to self." But, he wondered why I had not told him that it would need to happen *every day*!

If you're a caregiver, you'll need to "die to self" every day, not just on the days when you feel like it. And while you're putting the other person's needs ahead of your own, please don't forget that God has given you the opportunity for service as a means of fulfilling His plan and revealing His glory.

So, if you genuinely seek to discover God's unfolding purpose for your life, you must ask yourself this question: "How does God want me to serve Him today?"

Every single day of your life, including this one, the Lord will give you opportunities to serve Him by serving His children. Welcome those opportunities with open arms. They are His gift to you, His way of allowing you to see and touch part of the greatness of His kingdom.

How do you hold a hand? Of course, you can *physically* hold a hand when you comfort or pray with someone. But there are other ways to hold a hand, too. You can also "hold a hand" when you serve someone by visiting, by bringing food, by cleaning, or by giving time so a caregiver can rest or run errands. And, there is an even less obvious way of "hand-holding": by sharing your hardship with another. The sharing may even be painful when you are in the midst of a storm or in the deepest valley, but when you open your heart to others, you become a living testimony in and through the trial.

Because we are friends, because I am a physician, because Gini and I are going through this trial with cancer—but most of all, because we are Christians—Marcia from Australia called us. She had just found out her colon cancer has come back for the third time and that chemotherapy was failing. Marcia was having anxious thoughts and fears, and just wanted to talk to us and have us pray with her. She had asked the doctor how long she might be expected to live and was told that, while the timing is uncertain, she probably only has months.

Marcia wants to have rest, trust, and peace. I relayed that the Lord will help her make all the choices, such as continuing chemo or not. I relayed that she probably should not fly around the world searching for a cure. There is just the one choice: trusting the Lord.

Marcia asked Gini what she did when she found out her tumor had come back.

Gini answered that she accepted that her tumor would probably come back at some point, and that there were only certain things that could be done, and all is in the Lord's hands, not hers.

We prayed with Marcia and the Lord allowed us all

to have that peace and comfort that only He can provide. Here is her note the following morning:

> My world, our world, has been shaken these past couple of days. Like so many other people, I am now the one who has been given the news that the chemo is not working; instead, the tumors are growing and spreading.
>
> I would not be honest to say that I have it all worked out, have all my questions answered, know what we're doing, and have a total peace. Right now I'm struggling and holding on. Probably feeling like David in the Psalms who so often was in the pit of despair, but then gave it all to Jesus. It's a new road for our family once again. One thing I have learned is that we never know how we will deal with the circumstances given until we walk that road ourselves.
>
> "God is my refuge and my strength, an ever-present help in trouble. Therefore we will not fear, though the earth give way, and the mountains fall into the heart of the sea, though its waters roar and foam and the mountains quake with their surging." Psalm 46:1-3
>
> I will fight to rejoice in Him in all things. Yes, even when I don't know His thoughts because

they are not my thoughts or understand His ways because they are not my ways. My confidence is still in Him.

How are you depending on the Lord to hold your hand? Are you open to Him when He provides both visible and invisible opportunities? Do you see God holding your hand in a restaurant or airport when you experience one of those unexpected, God-appointed meetings with a friend or a stranger? Those meetings are timed to the very second, and they allow you to show other people a smile or a kind word in the midst of your trial—or theirs—by lifting their weary hands at just the right moment to give them strength and encouragement.

Do all the good you can. By all the means you can. In all the ways you can.
In all the places you can. At all the times you can. To all the people you can.
As long as ever you can.

—

John Wesley

LIGHT FOR OUR PATH FROM GOD'S WORD

But Moses' hands grew weary, so they took a stone and put it under him, and he sat on it, while Aaron and Hur held up his hands, one on one side, and the other on the other side. So his hands were steady until the going down of the sun.

Exodus 17:12 ESV

Therefore, God's chosen ones, holy and loved, put on heartfelt compassion, kindness, humility, gentleness, and patience.

Colossians 3:12 HCSB

But if anyone has the world's goods and sees his brother in need, yet closes his heart against him, how does God's love abide in him?

1 John 3:17 ESV

A kind man benefits himself, but a cruel man brings disaster on himself.

Proverbs 11:17 HCSB

And you shall consecrate the fiftieth year, and proclaim liberty throughout the land to all its inhabitants. It shall be a jubilee for you, when each of you shall return to his property and each of you shall return to his clan.

Leviticus 25:10 ESV

For you were once darkness, but now
you are light in the Lord. Walk as children
of light—for the fruit of the light results in
all goodness, righteousness, and truth—
discerning what is pleasing to the Lord.

—

Ephesians 5:8-10 HCSB

MORE IMPORTANT IDEAS ABOUT
CARING FOR OTHERS

A Christian is a perfectly free lord of all, subject to none. A Christian is a perfectly dutiful servant of all, subject to all.

Martin Luther

People don't care how much you know until they know how much you care.

John Maxwell

The most eloquent prayer is the prayer through hands that heal and bless. The highest form of worship is the worship of unselfish Christian service. The greatest form of praise is the sound of consecrated feet seeking out the lost and helpless.

Billy Graham

The greatest thing a man can do for his Heavenly Father is to be kind to some of His other children.

Henry Drummond

The measure of a man is not how many people he has serving him. It's how many people he, himself, can serve.

D. L. Moody

GINI'S JOURNEY

Hand-Holding

In the months since her operation, Gini and I have spent many happy hours looking at old photo albums and talking about various aspects of our lives apart and our life together.

We have received visitors, read the CaringBridge guestbook, poured over cards and e-mails, and received phone calls from family and friends. All these things have brought up memories of previous days. We have marveled at the way the Lord has allowed us to hold hands through all the years of courtship and marriage, now into our fiftieth year, truly a year of jubilee! And, we know that God will continue to hold our hands throughout this journey on earth as aliens and strangers.

Gini and I take hand-holding very seriously. Sometimes, I hold her hand to help her keep her balance as she walks through the house. At times, we simply sit, hold hands, and talk. On one occasion, she was quite sick, and I was letting her rest. As I came to check on her, she softly said, "I know you are busy doing something, but could you just hold my hand?" As you can imagine, I cried a bucketful of tears as we held hands! Although I certainly have missed quite a few hand-holding opportunities over the years "doing something," I try never to miss them now. And, since I am an optimistic and a cup-half-full person, I am just happy to have her make the request, and I'm blessed to be available to offer my hand in return.

Our hand-holding sessions are very precious to us both. Perhaps, they're more precious now than ever because we sense even more the strong right hand of the Lord taking our hand in His. He will hold our hand when we take the last step of this earthly life, leading us to our heavenly home.

Below are the fitting lyrics to one of Gini's favorite hymns, written by Thomas M. Dorsey in 1932.

PRECIOUS LORD, TAKE MY HAND

Precious Lord, take my hand,
Lead me on, let me stand,
I am tired, I am weak, I am worn.
Through the storm, through the night,
Lead me on to the light,
Take my hand precious Lord, lead me home.

When my way grows drear,
Precious Lord linger near,
When my life is almost gone.

Hear my cry, hear my call,
Hold my hand lest I fall,
Take my hand precious Lord, lead me home.

When the darkness appears,
And the night draws near,
And the day is past and gone.
At the river I stand,
Guide my feet, hold my hand,
Take my hand precious Lord, lead me home.

Precious Lord, take my hand,
Lead me on, let me stand,
I'm tired, I'm weak, I'm lone.
Through the storm, through the night,
Lead me on to the light,
Take my hand precious Lord, lead me home.

CHAPTER 19

—~—

Love Is Much More Than Just Sex

And now abide faith, hope, love, these three;
but the greatest of these is love.

—

1 Corinthians 13:13 NKJV

A LESSON FOR THE JOURNEY

—~—

The world's view of marital love often focuses
on sexual satisfaction. Serious illness or aging
often changes the way that couples react to each
other physically. So, it's important to remember
that genuine love is not just sex.

Why would I include a chapter on "sex" in a Christian book that deals with trials and death? I've chosen to address this important topic, a proverbial "elephant in the room," for one simple reason: I think it can help married couples going through progressive illnesses *or* sudden disabilities. And the fact is, *all* married couples must face sexual changes—to varying degrees—that occur with aging or with the disappointments they may feel about themselves or their spouses.

I believe my observations are helpful as a physician and a husband, and while this is a difficult chapter for me to write, I trust that it is appropriate. So, let me begin by recalling advice I received half a century ago.

As a young man, my grandfather told me that my love for Gini would, at least initially, be more sexually-oriented. But, I was also advised that those feelings would change in time. Now, after experiencing many years of marital joy, I can tell you that the advice I received 50 years ago was, and still is, true. Love is more than sex.

While early in marriage, our physical expression of love was satisfying and rewarding, Gini and I gradually changed our emphasis from physical love to a much deeper kind: the true love of God that is manifest in His definition of marriage, including, but certainly not limited to, sex. We understood that in every marriage, times of abstaining from sexual relations are appropriate. But we also knew that neither husband nor wife should ever hold the marriage bed hostage in any way (see 1 Corinthians 7:5).

For younger couples, the time of "abstaining" is sometimes measured in a few days. For more mature husbands and wives, abstinence is sometimes measured in days or weeks. But abstinence takes on a totally different meaning when a spouse experiences a serious illness, or an accident, or a loss of mental functioning that may result in permanent disability. Under such circumstances, the waiting may last years, or decades, or a lifetime.

We learned that, while our desires and abilities gradually diminished over time, our love kept growing stronger. Nonetheless, we were not prepared for the *sudden* change that occurred in our sexual life any more than we were prepared for any of our other trials that arrived without warning.

God's grace allowed us to already be slowing down; however, this change in our physical relationship was, all the same, abrupt. And, like many other couples, the sudden impact of that change was shocking, especially when we came to realize that her "new normal" would probably last for the rest of our married lives. For you see, the part of the brain attacked by her tumor included areas of emotions and connection. This fact, plus the stresses of chemotherapy and radiation, left Gini with physical and cognitive limitations that we simply cannot repair. So, she and I have agreed that we will love one another deeply and that our love will endure, and grow, *without* the sexual joys that we so treasured before her surgery.

We have many memories, of course. But now, a squeeze of a hand, a glance of the eyes, holding hands and hugging, is a very sufficient, rich, and warm experience because of the exceeding love of God that He has poured into us. I know that Gini still loves me very deeply, and I find that I fall more in love with her each day that the Lord allows her to remain on this earth with me, able to converse and to connect. But, I do and will love her just as much when she *cannot* converse and connect.

For you see, the Lord continues to meet *all* our needs through His Son, Christ Jesus. Jesus is sufficient for our lives *and* for our marriage.

Beloved, let us love one another,
for love is from God, and whoever loves
has been born of God and knows God.

—

1 John 4:7 ESV

LIGHT FOR OUR PATH FROM GOD'S WORD

Therefore a man shall leave his father and mother and be joined to his wife, and they shall become one flesh.

Genesis 2:24 NKJV

Marriage should be honored by all, and the marriage bed kept pure, for God will judge the adulterer and all the sexually immoral.

Hebrews 13:4 NIV

Let us behave decently, as in the daytime, not in carousing and drunkenness, not in sexual immorality and debauchery, not in dissension and jealousy.

Romans 13:13 NIV

You say, "Food for the stomach and the stomach for food, and God will destroy them both." The body, however, is not meant for sexual immorality but for the Lord, and the Lord for the body.

1 Corinthians 6:13 NIV

Flee from sexual immorality. All other sins a person commits are outside the body, but whoever sins sexually, sins against their own body.

1 Corinthians 6:18 NIV

MORE IMPORTANT IDEAS ABOUT MARRIAGE

Marriage is a divine institution, founded by God. Society did not make the first marriage; God did.

Billy Graham

The institution of marriage has been a sacred bond of fidelity between a man and a woman in every culture throughout recorded history. The pledge of loyalty and mutual support represented by marriage vows is a promise of commitment that extends to every aspect of life.

James Dobson

A man and woman should choose each other for life for the simple reason that a long life is barely enough time for a man and woman to understand each other, and to understand is to love.

George Truett

The real mystery of marriage is not that husband and wife love each other so much that they can find God in each other's lives, but that God loves them so much that they can discover each other more and more as living reminders of God's presence.

Henri Nouwen

Those who abandon ship the first time it enters a storm miss the calm beyond. And the rougher the storms weathered together, the deeper and stronger real love grows.

Ruth Bell Graham

I came to know and love Gene and Gini after the diagnosis of her tumor. Gene (and Gini) stepped into the story God is writing in all our lives as he joined a short-term mission trip to Liberia, Africa, with his granddaughter. As a leader of that team, I got to know both Gene and Gini. I realized that I was actually sitting on the front row watching a love story paralleling none I had ever seen. For you see, their love for each truly represents the type of love Paul described in 1 Corinthians 13:4-7. Their love is patient and kind; it does not envy or boast. It is not arrogant or rude, doesn't insist on its own way, and is not irritable or resentful. It doesn't rejoice at wrongdoing, but rejoices with the truth. It bears all things, believes all things, hopes all things, endures all things. Their love for each other during a most challenging time has been a source of encouragement and joy for me. After all, how many husbands would paint their wives nails to match the dress he helped her select at the mall? That is real love!

In His love, Karen Rigsby

GINI'S JOURNEY

*Love, Respect, and Trust
Never Go Out of Style*

I came across a recent survey that described the qualities men and women value most in the opposite sex. For men, that quality is *trustworthiness*. Women, on the other hand, are looking for men they can *respect*. The best relationships—and the best marriages—are still built upon a foundation of trust and mutual respect. That's just the kind of marriage Gini and I have. We love each other; we respect each other, and we trust each other. We know the Lord has blessed us in the past and that He continues to do so every day.

I don't need to tell you that the media has changed quite a bit since Gini and I first met. Fifty years ago, the popular media still honored marriage. But, it's not that way anymore. Today, the media seems to be working around the clock in an attempt to redefine what it means to be in a "physical relationship" and what it means to be married.

When it comes to marriage, society usually portrays sex, not as a beautiful thing to be treasured only between man and wife, but instead as a "hook up" or "recreational" activity between "two consenting adults" whether they are married or not. Such messages are dangerous because they are clearly contrary to God's Word.

As she reflected on our married life, Gini had these thoughts:

Looking back on our marriage, Gene and I have had a rich relationship blessed by God, and I think it is mostly because God helped us follow His design for marriage. Our marriage was not perfect; we both had our times of struggles with temptations of all kinds, the difficulties that all marriages struggle with. I cannot list or remember all of the ways that God helped both of us, but we saw God's principles were to keep our marriage vows and commitment as specific guidelines, not general advice or vague suggestions. Some specific examples: We kept one another accountable. We had passwords for the other, we used each other's cell phones, but we did not need to check because we trusted each other. We prayed for one another and for many specific temptations, so that we knew we could remain faithful to one another. In order to repair our horizontal relationship with one another, we both knew we needed to repair our vertical relationship, seeking closeness to God individually and together. I also concentrated on respecting Gene as well as loving him. I also saw Gene's love for me in addition to his respect for me in every way.

So, if you're single, Gini and I pray that you will make God's Word the ultimate authority over every aspect of your dating life, including the very wise choice to refrain from sex until after you're married. I know you will be blessed.

And if you're already married, Gini and I pray that you and your spouse will experience the same trust, respect, and love that we've shared for 50 years. She truly is the wife of my life.

The husband should give to his wife her conjugal rights,
and likewise the wife to her husband. For the wife does not
have authority over her own body, but the husband does.
Likewise the husband does not have authority over his
own body, but the wife does. Do not deprive one another,
except perhaps by agreement for a limited time, that you
may devote yourselves to prayer; but then come together
again, so that Satan may not tempt you because
of your lack of self-control.

—

1 Corinthians 7:3-5 ESV

CHAPTER 20

—❧—

It's a Privilege to Worship

I was glad when they said unto me,
Let us go into the house of the LORD.

—

Psalm 122:1 KJV

A LESSON FOR THE JOURNEY

—❧—

God intends for you to worship Him with
a grateful heart and willing hands.
So, don't ever think of worship as a burden;
think of it as a privilege.

Sundays were always Gini's favorite day of the week. She loved being with the body of believers and worshipping together in church. Whenever we traveled, we tried never to miss worshipping on Sunday. Recently, when her brother Virg was visiting, Gini was confused as to the day of the week, and for several days she kept thinking it was Sunday. She took our "correction" well, but on one occasion she said, "You know, not everyone gets a week of seven Sundays!"

After Gini's operation, I wondered when—perhaps I should use the word "if"—the two of us would worship together in church again. Never to sit beside one another in church? Not to both hear God's Word taught from one of my top-10 preachers/teachers, Patrick Miller. It was a disconcerting thought. But God was gracious, and that day came sooner than expected. Below is an excerpt from a CaringBridge post I made on that glorious day, less than two months after she was diagnosed with her brain cancer:

SUNDAY, MAY 1, 2011
WHAT A PRIVILEGE TO WORSHIP!

With His strength, we were able to go to church. We were only a little late and so enjoyed being able to sing, pray, and hear God's Word read and preached.

The sermon was on Luke 9:1-9 and the application to us was that, just as the disciples, we have power and authority (with the help of the Holy Spirit in us) to proclaim the gospel and to minister in His name (word and deed). We depend on God's provision and His power to meet any resistance.

Now we will enjoy the remainder of our Sabbath. We will rest spiritually and physically, knowing we can travel light (Luke 9:3) and have the full armor of God to fight all battles (Ephesians 6:10-20).

Our prayer for you is the same—that these truths would be applied to your heart, as you also rest and trust in the Lord this day and every day. We are getting the routines down but it is a moving target of sorts. Focusing is hard to do and fatigue sets in quickly but we have a great God as well as the privilege of being called His children.

Psalm 96:4-9 "For great is the LORD, and greatly to be praised; He is to be feared above all gods . . . but the LORD made the heavens. Splendor and majesty are before Him; strength and beauty are in His sanctuary. Ascribe to the LORD, O families of the peoples, ascribe to the LORD glory and strength! Ascribe to the LORD the glory due His

name; bring an offering, and come into His courts!
Worship the LORD in the splendor of holiness;
tremble before Him, all the earth."

What a joy it was to worship the Lord in our congregation with Gini that day. And, how thankful I am for all the worship services we've experienced together in and out of church.

Some people may tell you that they don't engage in worship. Don't believe them. All of mankind worships *something*. The question is not *whether* we worship, but *what* we worship. My prayer for you is that you will choose to worship God. And, I pray that you will worship Him seven days a week, not just on Sunday mornings. For Gini and me, worshipping is holding hands when we pray, helping others in the Lord's name, studying His Word, discipling others, seeing a sunset or a storm, not to mention those wonderful days when we sang hymns together as she played the piano.

Worship is, indeed, a privilege. Please don't ever take it for granted. Instead, look upon worship as gift from above, an opportunity to express your love for the Lord and to experience His love for you. Read and meditate on Psalm 19. Worship as the Lord shows you His work in creation, and then declares that His Word guides us in the work He is doing through us. Then, consider the final words of that

Psalm: "Let the words of my mouth and the meditation of my heart be acceptable in your sight, O Lord, my rock and my redeemer" (ESV).

Remember to worship God your Father, not just with words, but also with deeds. Honor Him; praise Him, and obey Him. Seek His purpose and His will for your day and your life. Put Him first. Always first.

So that at the name of Jesus every knee should bow—of those who are in heaven and on earth and under the earth—and every tongue should confess that Jesus Christ is Lord, to the glory of God the Father.

—

Philippians 2:10-11 HCSB

LIGHT FROM OUR PATH FROM GOD'S WORD

But an hour is coming, and is now here, when the true worshipers will worship the Father in spirit and truth. Yes, the Father wants such people to worship Him. God is Spirit, and those who worship Him must worship in spirit and truth.

John 4:23-24 HCSB

For where two or three are gathered together in My name, I am there among them.

Matthew 18:20 HCSB

Enter into his gates with thanksgiving, and into his courts with praise: be thankful unto him, and bless his name.

Psalm 100:4 KJV

All the earth shall worship You and sing praises to You; they shall sing praises to Your name.

Psalm 66:4 NKJV

But seek first the kingdom of God and His righteousness, and all these things shall be added to you.

Matthew 6:33 NKJV

But it is good for me to draw near to God: I have put my trust in the Lord GOD....

Psalm 73:28 KJV

More Important Ideas About Worship

Ay, call it holy ground, / The soil where first they trod!
They have left unstained what there they found—Freedom
to worship God.

Felicia Hermans

Worship is spiritual. Our worship must be more than just
outward expression, it must also take place in our spirits.

Franklin Graham

God asks that we worship Him with our concentrated
minds as well as with our wills and emotions. A divided
and scattered mind is not effective.

Catherine Marshall

It is impossible to worship God and remain unchanged.

Henry Blackaby

Each time, before you intercede, be quiet first and worship
God in His glory. Think of what He can do and how He
delights to hear the prayers of His redeemed people. Think
of your place and privilege in Christ, and expect great
things!

Andrew Murray

Praise Him! Praise Him!
Tell of His excellent greatness.
Praise Him! Praise Him!
Ever in joyful song!

—

Fanny Crosby

GINI'S JOURNEY

Our Family's Worship Experience

Through the years, the blessing of worship has been a priority for Gini, for me, and for our family. Let me give you a few examples.

Because of my training years, we worshipped in new churches in our new places. Finding a new church and developing new friendships was a joy.

Our oldest daughter, Becky, commented, "My memories are of all the different churches we attended whenever we moved, or when you took us with you to out-of-town pathology meetings. I still love finding a church to go to on Sunday wherever I am because of those memories. Wherever I went, that was one of my first goals: I wanted to find a church. That has always been the first place I looked for friends and 'family.' It was a lesson I learned from both of you."

During our 35 years of living in Anderson, Gini and I saw that the Lord had actually been preparing and "training" us to help with new churches. So we have helped in "planting" four new churches. One of these was a church that had just begun services when we arrived to practice pathology in Australia. The Lord provided a church for us that was within walking distance from our apartment in Brisbane, a city of two million!

Early days in a new church mean one thing for sure: Everyone involved has duties that they may not feel called to do, or may not feel adequate to perform. Serving the Lord is more than feelings, and worshipping Him is not sitting as a spectator. It is hearing God's Word and responding to His call on our lives.

The sacrifices and the "training" the Lord puts us through are not only what He has called us to do, but also ways that He can bear fruit through our efforts. Gini often played the piano, taught Sunday school, and prepared the bulletins. I, along with some of the other men were the elders; we often taught more than just Sunday school; sometimes we preached if no pastor was available. Our girls sang in the choir (or sometimes solo) and helped with children. To say that we were "relieved" when our churches became large enough to have separate people serving in all these places is an understatement. But the Lord did not let us rest very long before providing another "opportunity."

There were times during our involvement in church plants when all was not smooth. Besides the usual trials of strengthening and growing a new congregation, we sometimes experienced division, and people sometimes left the church. These divisions were always disappointing, and often I could not see how God could permit it or make it right. But in the end, the Lord often allowed another church plant or another ministry to flourish. New and younger leadership arose, and both Gini and I came to see that again the Lord was at work, raising up the next generation.

Another area of worshipping, and working, for the Lord has been our experience on short-term mission trips. You have read that the Lord brought both of us to Christ on such a trip. Many more have chosen to accept Christ on such trips, and we have seen our children blessed by their own mission experiences. On one, I watched the Lord at work in Wesley, one of our foster sons. And just this past summer, I accompanied my granddaughter Elizabeth to Liberia to serve the Lord among Muslim children and adults.

Another grandson, McCray, has recently gone to Uganda. What a privilege to work for, and worship the Lord, in all the world. And, what a delight it is to see Him passing the baton. For Gini and me, this is another joy of seeing our children and grandchildren walking in the truth.

Last year we discovered God was also "training" us for helping with yet another new church, this time in downtown Anderson. It's a place where we can help meet the needs of those less fortunate. This is our current church; we are older and not the primary leaders—sometimes,

Gini arrives in a wheelchair. But we still rejoice in the opportunity of worshipping and serving our great Savior, Lord, and Treasure, however we can, wherever He leads.

Finally, here's a message Gini and I received from two dear church friends who attended church with us for years and then moved away from Anderson. This note reminds me that it is not only important to *attend* church, but it is also important to *invite* other people to attend church.

Dear Gene,

You and Gini were the ones who kept inviting us to church when we were looking for a new church home. Thank you for your perseverance and hospitality. God allowed you to show us the marvelous grace He has.

Jeanne and Mike

—•~•—

CHAPTER 21

You Are the Light

For God has not given us a spirit of fear and timidity, but of power, love, and self-discipline. So you must never be ashamed to tell others about our Lord.

—

2 Timothy 1:7-8 NLT

A LESSON FOR THE JOURNEY
—•~•—

The story of *your* faith is vitally important, and God wants you to share it.

Over the years, God granted Gini and me numerous opportunities for international travel, so that He might use us up for His glory. Many were mission trips that provided profound blessings for us as we shared God's message wherever we went. On one of those trips, a special time in Korea, our lives were forever changed, as we realized that the Lord was calling us to a higher level of commitment. God not only called us to Himself and granted us salvation, but He also showed us that, with His power, we could share His light in ways that would be impossible without Him.

In the first chapter of James, we are told that "Every good gift and every perfect gift is from above, coming down from the Father of lights." And, in the same chapter, we are instructed to "be doers of the word, and not hearers only, deceiving yourselves."

The Lord shines light in our darkness so that we can clearly see His gifts, and so that we can know how best to use those gifts. As we reflect His light, He is asking each of us to put that light to use where it will shine best. He wants us to use our time, our talents, our words, and our actions to honor Him and to tell of the marvelous things He has done.

We live in a world that is in desperate need of Christ's message. So, those of us who are Christians should be willing to talk about the things that Jesus has done *for us*. But sometimes, because of our shyness or insecurities, we may be hesitant to share our experiences. On other occasions, we may believe that we're simply "too busy" to share the Good News of our Savior because we have "other things" we to need to do.

If you have Jesus in your heart, you know it, and you also know how He has transformed your life. And to-day, perhaps this very moment, someone near you may be touched by your testimony. Ask Him to allow you to see those God-appointed moments. I pray that today you will share the Good News of Jesus Christ with someone, whether a family member, a friend, or a complete stranger. This day is the perfect time to share your testimony be-cause tomorrow may simply be too late.

How many people
have you made homesick for God?

—

Oswald Chambers

LIGHT FOR OUR PATH FROM GOD'S WORD

But you are a chosen generation, a royal priesthood, a holy nation, His own special people, that you may proclaim the praises of Him who called you out of darkness into His marvelous light.

1 Peter 2:9 NKJV

You are the light of the world. A city set on a hill cannot be hidden. Nor do people light a lamp and put it under a basket, but on a stand, and it gives light to all in the house. In the same way, let your light shine before others, so that they may see your good works and give glory to your Father who is in heaven.

Matthew 5:14-15 ESV

But sanctify the Lord God in your hearts, and always be ready to give a defense to everyone who asks you a reason for the hope that is in you.

1 Peter 3:15 HCSB

But as for me, I will never boast about anything except the cross of our Lord Jesus Christ, through whom the world has been crucified to me, and I to the world.

Galatians 6:14 HCSB

For I decided to know nothing among you except Jesus Christ and him crucified.

1 Corinthians 2:2 ESV

And I say to you, anyone who acknowledges Me before men, the Son of Man will also acknowledge him before the angels of God; but whoever denies Me before men will be denied before the angels of God.

Luke 12:8-9 HCSB

Then He said to them, "Go into all the world and preach the gospel to the whole creation."

Mark 16:15 HCSB

I will also make you a light for the nations, to be My salvation to the ends of the earth.

Isaiah 49:6 HCSB

How beautiful upon the mountains are the feet of him who brings good news, who publishes peace, who brings good news of happiness, who publishes salvation, who says to Zion, "Your God reigns."

Isaiah 52:7 ESV

MORE IMPORTANT IDEAS ABOUT
YOUR TESTIMONY

Send the light, the blessed gospel light; let it shine from shore to shore!

Charles H. Gabriel

It's a joy to share my faith. I've found something so special that I want others to share in it. When something is that close to your heart, share it.

Michael Chang

Christianity spread rapidly during the first century because all Christians saw themselves as responsible for disseminating the gospel.

Erwin Lutzer

There is nothing more appealing or convincing to a watching world than to hear the testimony of someone who has just been with Jesus.

Henry Blackaby

We need to talk to God about people, then talk to people about God.

Dieter Zander

GINI'S JOURNEY

Many Ways to Share the Message

There are many ways to share the Lord's message with the world. Sometimes, we can share that message in person, but that's not always possible. That's why Gini and I have been blessed to know, to pray for, and to support missionaries who have dedicated their lives to the glorious task of sharing Christ's message in many distant lands.

Two such missionaries are John and Sue Burch. Below is an excerpt from a note they sent to Gini and me:

Dear Gene and Gini,

Before we leave for Belgium to serve as mentors for new missionaries in cross-cultural training (and then return soon to Asia and Australia), I wanted to make sure we got a note off to you.

You have been in our prayers over the last year. We have been blessed, not only by your sharing of your journey with Gini's cancer, but also by your journey of love. Your relationship with each other and with our Lord has been such a sweet encouragement to us.

Thank you for your faithful and generous giving to our support and ministry, too! So many blessings!

Praying Still,
John and Sue

Despite the many changes that have resulted from her cancer, Gini is still ministering to her family and friends. She is ministering in different ways now. Sometimes, she'll recite a Bible verse from memory or join in on a song; on other occasions, she'll share a smile or say only a few words. But perhaps her greatest testimony is simply her life: the example that she set in the past *and* the example she sets today as Jesus the Light of the world, reflects from her.

Gini has built her life on an unshakeable faith, a faith that is stronger than fear, and stronger than cancer. Despite everything she has endured, Christ in her life remains her greatest testimony. And it's a beautiful thing to behold.

I recently picked up Gini's current Bible containing hundreds of notes written over the past 15 years. Here are some excerpts preceded by their location. These passages give me a window to see how God has been preparing both of us for these current days. He is merciful and gracious to provide and may He do and continue to do the same for you.

Ecclesiastes 3: Agonizing limitations are God's gifts; focus on God's sovereignty, not on time and circumstances.

Job 42:12: The former days were not better than these; the end is better than the beginning.

Ecclesiastes 11:4: Don't focus on things you can't control—labor and trust God for the result (see John 12:23-26).

Ecclesiastes 11:9: Find God early in life and follow Him all your days.

Ecclesiastes 12:6-7: "If I die before I wake…" What should I do today? No regrets. Be fruitful. Remember my vows. Keep integrity. Worship and praise the Lord.

Isaiah 6:5: I cannot depend on my own "natural" ability.

Isaiah 6:5-13: Seeing my own sinfulness and that of my culture helps me realize God's great mercy to me, THE sinner (see Luke 18:13).

John 9:25: I was blind and could not see, but now I see and believe! To see or not to see, that is the question.

Isaiah 6: My prayer: "Send me, O God. Deliver me from small, peripheral prayers. You are Lord of the nations. The whole earth is full of Your glory. Deliver me from my puny, self-absorbed priority list. Let me live freely and generously, giving of my material wealth to serve those in need. Deliver me from my addiction to security and self-preservation. I'm at Your disposal to take the good news of forgiveness through Jesus Christ across the street or across the world. Send me."

Jesus made Himself known
to His own, and if others
are to hear about Him today,
you and I must tell them.

—

Vance Havner

CHAPTER 22

—⌘—

A Legacy of Love

I have no greater joy than this:
to hear that my children are walking in the truth.

—

3 John 1:4 HCSB

A LESSON FOR THE JOURNEY

—⌘—

Your family members *and* your extended
family are God's gift to you.
Treasure them and be grateful.

Gini and I have always been so very grateful for our family *and* for the extended family of faith that the Lord has placed along our path. She and I raised three biological daughters, and God has blessed us with eight grandchildren who all profess Christ as their Lord and Savior. We know not only that our children are a gift from the Lord, we also praise Him for their loving witness to their children and so many others, for their willingness to serve Him, and for the way the Lord is using them.

For Gini's sixty-fifth birthday, the grandchildren each wrote her a note, and certain excerpts I want you to read. You will see that they know the *Truth*, and that God is already at work in the next generation.

"You taught me the story of the Bible using the 'Walk Through.' I groaned while doing it, but now I have reaped the lush benefits. You also taught me about the Bible and Christ in a novel yet special way. You gave me something I can remember forever and always." —Ben

"When I was 4, I accepted Jesus as I sat with my Mom after a Backyard Bible Club held at our house. Through Bible classes at school, I have learned about God and how to serve Him."
—Stephen

"Since I first met Jesus at age 3, I wanted to know Christ and learn to love Him the way He loves me. Last year I really 'got' that repent means to turn from your ways and do or go the opposite. I have done this and do it daily. I try not to worry about the future by reminding myself of His promise from Philippians 4. I thank you for teaching me to always walk with Christ so that He might be seen through me—when we were walking together on the beach just before the sun went down for the night." —Elizabeth

"I remember the hand motions to help outline the Bible, and mornings with you at the beach. We would have a Bible time and you taught me how easy it is to find God in everything and how everything is going to work out for His purpose. You helped me see the beauty of heaven and earth and how simple acts can praise God." —Baillie

"I was 4 and in my bedroom with my Mom and Dad and my two brothers. I said what Dad suggested, and became a Christian. Being a Christian means that I believe in Jesus and that He died for me and that I am going to heaven." —McCray

"I thought it would be fun to sew a frog and you helped me with your sewing machine. I know how I did such a great job, you were a great teacher. You also teach me about the Bible and how to be a Christian and that helps me out a lot. You are a gift from God. Know you are loved." —Sam

"I trusted Jesus when I was 4. I was in Atlanta. I was sitting on a red chair. I love you." —Campbell

"When I was 4, I became a Christian. I was in bed and Mom asked me if I brushed my teeth. I lied and felt bad. I asked if I was going to hell. I asked Jesus into my heart." —Chandler

We were also blessed to raise four foster boys who were part of a family of eight children. So we now have an additional seven grandchildren from our foster sons along with many spiritual grandchildren from all of the men and women God has brought into our lives over the years. Truly, our spiritual family extends throughout the world, reflecting Gini's life verse: 3 John 4.

But, our *real* family is much larger than the men, women, boys and girls I've described above. You see, we also belong to God's family, and, if you're a Christian, you, too, are a part of our family! We've all been adopted *by* God.

John 1:12-13 makes this promise: "But to all who did receive him, who believed in his name, he gave the right to become children of God, who were born, not of blood nor of the will of the flesh nor of the will of man, but of God."

What a wonderful privilege to be called the children of God! Being adopted into the Lord's family means that we are His eternally. What a joy; what a gift; what a blessing!

A loving family, whether biological or otherwise, is a priceless gift from above. So today, my prayer for you is simple. I pray that you will treasure your biological family, your extended family, and your adoptive family in Christ. And, I pray that you will place God squarely at the center of your marriage, your family, and your life.

LIGHT FOR OUR PATH FROM GOD'S WORD

Unless the Lord builds a house, its builders labor over it in vain.

Psalm 127:1 HCSB

Beyond all these things put on love, which is the perfect bond of unity.

Colossians 3:14 NASB

Above all, love each other deeply, because love covers over a multitude of sins.

1 Peter 4:8 NIV

The one who loves his brother remains in the light, and there is no cause for stumbling in him.

1 John 2:10 HCSB

I pray that you, being rooted and firmly established in love, may be able to comprehend with all the saints what is the breadth and width, height and depth, and to know the Messiah's love that surpasses knowledge, so you may be filled with all the fullness of God.

Ephesians 3:17-19 HCSB

This is My commandment, that you love one another as I have loved you.

John 15:12 NKJV

Love must be without hypocrisy.
Detest evil; cling to what is good.
Show family affection to one another
with brotherly love. Outdo one another
in showing honor.

—

Romans 12:9-10 HCSB

MORE IMPORTANT IDEAS ABOUT
CARING FOR FAMILY AND FRIENDS

Every Christian family ought to be, as it were, a little church, consecrated to Christ, and wholly influenced and governed by His rules.

Jonathan Edwards

If Christ is in your house, your neighbors will soon know it.

D. L. Moody

It is impossible to overstate the need for prayer in family life.

James Dobson

Employ whatever God has entrusted you with, in doing good, all possible good, in every possible kind and degree.

John Wesley

The glory of friendship is not the outstretched hand, or the kindly smile, or the joy of companionship. It is the spiritual inspiration that comes to one when he discovers that someone else believes in him and is willing to trust him with his friendship.

Corrie ten Boom

GINI'S JOURNEY

Still Witnessing

How blessed we have been by our family. Below is a note from the in-laws of our youngest daughter, Heather. We have treasured our long friendship with Paul and Tonia, as you can tell from the letter they sent after a recent visit:

Dear Gene and Gini,

How we loved our time with you. Thank you for your hospitality; it was worth every mile we traveled! We so enjoyed just sitting with you and being together.

Your illness, Gini, has a way of making the most important things in life (relationships) come into focus. It was so neat to see you, Gene, in your sweet servant role with Gini. What a great model for us and all your friends and family.

We're so thankful for our over 20 years of friendship. To have you and Gene as such dear friends, with such special times together, has been one of the great treats of our lives.

Gini, I think we are most thankful for the way you mothered your girls and loved your husband, because Heather was so influenced by you, and now she is such a good wife to Rod, and terrific mother and spiritual example to her three sons.

We have been so blessed by Rod's marriage to Heather. It makes me realize that we need to be praying not only for wonderful godly wives for the three boys, but also for godly mothers raising those girls.

Thank you for your life and influence to all of us. We love you.

Paul and Tonia

This is another example of how Gini's influence on our family has been, and continues to be, enormous. And, amazingly, she's *still* making a difference today, despite everything she's been through.

The lesson we can learn from Gini is simply this: When we become living witnesses for Christ, we never know *whom* we will touch, or what kind of *miracles* the Lord will perform using us as a tool in His hand. Our every thought, word, and action today, and every day, have eternal consequences.

CHAPTER 23

—⦿—

Celebrating, and Remembering, the Milestones

A joyful heart is good medicine,
but a broken spirit dries up the bones.

—

Proverbs 17:22 NASB

A LESSON FOR THE JOURNEY

—⦿—

Throughout your life, you will experience
many happy milestones.
God wants you to celebrate them.

We've always enjoyed annual family events, such as holidays, our special week at the beach each summer with the girls and their families, birthdays, and anniversaries. But, after Gini's surgery, each milestone has become even more precious to us. Her illness has provided an ever-present reminder that, because our days here on this earth are numbered, each day, and each milestone, is a gift of incalculable value.

The Bible makes much of milestones such as yearly feasts, including the shedding of the blood of a lamb at Passover that allowed the firstborn sons to live (see Exodus 12). The purpose of these milestones is straightforward: to be mindful of what God has done *and* what He continues to do for His people. Sometimes these milestones were marked by annual celebrations. In other instances, they were memorialized by physical monuments.

Memorial stones were left to remember how God helped the Israelites cross over the River Jordan at flood stage (Joshua 4:1-7):

> *Now when all the nation had finished crossing the Jordan, the LORD spoke to Joshua, saying, "Take . . . one man from each tribe, and command them, saying, 'Take up for yourselves twelve stones from here out of the middle of the Jordan, from the place where the priests' feet are standing firm, and carry them over*

with you and lay them down in the lodging place where you will lodge tonight. . . .' So these stones shall become a memorial to the sons of Israel forever."

And, in the seventh chapter of 1 Samuel, another memorial was created. After a long period of struggle resulting from their disobedience, the Israelites had repented and made Samuel their priest and judge. God blessed the Israelites under Samuel's leadership, and he created a milestone to commemorate the Lord's mercy: "Then Samuel took a stone and set it up between Mizpah and Shen, and called its name Ebenezer, saying, 'Thus, the Lord has helped us'" (v. 12).

Samuel placed this large stone at the very spot where the Israelites' restoration began. Then, he publicly dedicated it as a monument to God's help, to God's faithfulness, and to God's eternal covenant. As the people continued with their daily lives, the stone remained, visible to all who passed by, as a continual reminder of judgment and repentance, of mercy and restoration.

The Ebenezer Stone represented a fresh beginning, a reversal for God's people. The monument also reminded the people about their ever-present God, that His mercies are everlasting, and that His covenant endures forever.

In a similar way, we are reminded how the Lord has helped us. Jane, one of our older friends, tells us she prays for us each day, and I asked her how she remembers. She said, "I have a place in my house where I have placed a reminder, so each time I look or walk by, I stop to pray for you both."

I realized that we have a dish with some coffee beans sitting on a little table, and I do the same thing. They are to remind us to be the aroma of Christ each day. But, each time I go by or see the dish, I remember to pray for the teenage son and daughter of missionary friends who gave these coffee beans to us after a mission trip to Africa.

Some of our friends keep prayer journals where they record their requests to God and the answers that they receive. In this way, they can, from time to time, look back and review their walk with God. When they do, they are inevitably reminded of the Lord's help and faithfulness.

Prayer journals and physical reminders are a type of Ebenezer Stone. They keep us mindful that God does answer prayers and that He does guide our steps in accordance with His perfect plan. In 1 Peter 2, we are told that we are to be living stones to be built up into a spiritual house for a holy use. We are not to be just a memorial sitting beside the road; we are to be living milestones that people can see and interact with. This gives us the opportunity to speak to others for the purpose of proclaiming the Lord, and the sure hope of eternal life that is within us, in every thought, word, and deed—as we walk with fellow travelers along the path set before us.

So, my prayer for you today is this: I pray that you will celebrate your own family milestones with a grateful heart. Understand the privilege of being a living, breathing memorial stone of God's faithfulness. And, as you celebrate God's mercies and goodness, and as you reach additional milestones on your journey, I pray that you will find ways to bless others as you remember what God has done for you.

Think of the blessings we so easily
take for granted: Life itself; preservation
from danger; every bit of health we enjoy;
every hour of liberty; the ability to see,
to hear, to speak, to think, and to imagine
all this comes from the hand of God.

—

Billy Graham

LIGHT FOR OUR PATH FROM GOD'S WORD

This day shall be for you a memorial day, and you shall keep it as a feast to the Lord; throughout your generations, as a statute forever, you shall keep it as a feast.

Exodus 12:7 ESV

And it shall be to you as a sign on your hand and as a memorial between your eyes, that the law of the Lord may be in your mouth. For with a strong hand the Lord has brought you out of Egypt.

Exodus 13:9 ESV

As you come to him, a living stone rejected by men but in the sight of God chosen and precious, you yourselves like living stones are being built up as a spiritual house, to be a holy priesthood, to offer spiritual sacrifices acceptable to God through Jesus Christ.

1 Peter 2:4-5 ESV

The Lord has done great things for us; we are glad.

Psalm 126:3 NASB

A good and honest life is a blessed memorial.

Proverbs 10:7 MSG

In the day of prosperity be happy, but in the day of adversity consider—God has made the one as well as the other.

Ecclesiastes 7:14 NASB

Let the hearts of those who seek the Lord rejoice. Look to the Lord and his strength; seek his face always.

1 Chronicles 16:10-11 NIV

I will thank the Lord with all my heart; I will declare all Your wonderful works. I will rejoice and boast about You; I will sing about Your name, Most High.

Psalm 9:1-2 HCSB

So teach us to number our days, that we may gain a heart of wisdom.

Psalm 90:12 NKJV

Thou wilt show me the path of life: in thy presence is fulness of joy; at thy right hand there are pleasures for evermore.

Psalm 16:11 KJV

For the Lord is good; His mercy is everlasting, and His truth endures to all generations.

Psalm 100:5 NKJV

MORE IMPORTANT IDEAS ABOUT
MEMORIES, MILESTONES, AND GOD'S BLESSINGS

Remembered joys are never past.

James Montgomery

God gave us memories that we might have roses in December.

James Barrie

Lord, keep my memories green.

Charles Dickens

The past sharpens perspective, warns of pitfalls, and helps to point the way.

Dwight D. Eisenhower

Friends fill the memory with sweet thoughts.

Martha Washington

Memories are the key, not to the past, but to the future.

Corrie ten Boom

Oh! what a Savior, gracious to all, / Oh! how His blessings round us fall, / Gently to comfort, kindly to cheer, / Sleeping or waking, God is near.

Fanny Crosby

GINI'S JOURNEY

Memories

During the past two years, Gini and I have reflected on the life the Lord has given both of us on this earth—both separate and together—and on our many milestones: our meeting, falling in love, getting married, having three girls, then four foster sons, and many grandchildren.

While we continue our sojourn on this earth as strangers and pilgrims, we've stopped to look at old pictures and scrapbooks of our first years together, and we've praised the Lord for His many blessings. And, at Christmastime, we have been reminded time and again of our *spiritual* milestones as we've remembered the Gift who is our Savior and Lord. Most of all, we are grateful that He has saved us from our sins and that we know of the sure promise of eternal life with Him.

We have received countless e-mails, texts, calls, and notes of encouragement. And, we also received many messages telling us what the Lord has done through us. I told Gini that reading these messages is like hearing your own eulogy. But, while hearing these things does give us comfort and pride, that pride is not in ourselves, but praising the Lord for allowing us to get just a glimpse of some of what He has done. This is a privilege that many of us never hear or learn. May the Lord allow you to see how He is using each of you, even this day.

I have often written notes to others asking that the Lord bless them, not so they can be blessed only, but that they might be a blessing to everyone the Lord leads across their paths. This blessing is based on Genesis 12:2-3, expressing God's promise to Abraham. And now, after two years of struggling, suffering, surviving, and rejoicing, we reflect on how the Lord has, and continues, to bless us.

When Heather was engaged to Rod and visiting the seminary where they were going to live and study soon after their marriage, she became very anxious. She called me in the middle of the night, very fearful about her future. She recalls very clearly that my reassurance to her involved this idea of milestones. I encouraged her with the thought that God's faithfulness never changes, and that she would look back on this time of anxiety as a milestone of that faithfulness. I told her that she could look forward to adding many more "stones" of remembrance.

We pray that we will continue to be a blessing to you as we proclaim His truth and His saving grace in our lives along this journey with you, our fellow travelers. We are thankful to be able to make plans, but we can, and do, depend on the Lord to guide and direct each step.

—∾—

CHAPTER 24

Rejoice!

Weeping may endure for a night,
but joy comes in the morning.

—

Psalm 30:5 NKJV

A LESSON FOR THE JOURNEY

—∾—

Earthly pains are temporary and heavenly gifts
are eternal; you can be joyful,
even during difficult days.

Almost two years after being diagnosed with cancer, Gini and I returned to the Duke Medical Center for another follow-up test. I described the results in the following post:

Our Duke Brain Tumor Clinic doctor, Katy Peters, called and told us the PET scan on Gini has confirmed that there are two small spots of recurrent tumor (21 months after the first diagnosis). One is in the original tumor area and one is on the other side of her brain.

Although some of our previous treatment options cannot be used, she emphasized they are small and most patients respond to treatment. We are thankful that the Lord allows us to make diagnoses and discover treatments.

One aspect of all this is that, though no guarantees, there is every expectation that the areas of tumor are small and treatable. But we also know that Gini, or anyone needing such treatments, is not a percentage. Each patient either responds or does not respond, and that is also in the Lord's hands.

As I sit here writing this update note before returning to be with Gini and hold her hand and pray, I think of Job when he was going through his unbelievable trials; he said, "Blessed be the name of the Lord." And "Bless the Lord, O my soul and do not forget all His benefits" from Psalm 103:2. This will be our prayer right now too, as we pray our joy will continue to be from our gracious Lord, counterbalancing any sorrow, sadness, or other "downers" that might waft through.

In Romans 8:18, Paul makes this promise: "For I consider that the sufferings of this present time are not worth comparing with the glory that is to be revealed to us" (ESV). Since her surgery, Gini and I have trusted God's Word—through recovery, through rehabilitation, and through setbacks. On good days and hard days, we have clung tightly to the assurance of God's covenant. We have trusted that "the glory that will be revealed" will be shown to us in God's perfect time. And, when His glory is made known, it will make these difficult days pale by comparison.

The past two years have been a season for many tears, but also a season for much rejoicing. We have made the choice to rejoice and to be glad in all that the Lord does—and to be thankful for all that He allows in our lives—because we know it is for our good and for His glory.

We know that we need to see the joy, the love, and the peace that comes from evaluating our past and seeing what the Lord is doing in our lives, so we can then seek to live each day in the newness of the life we have in our relationship with Christ. By trusting Him, we know that the present day's troubles are temporary, but that His love for us is eternal. This knowledge gives us joy in the present and hope for our future, despite any co-existing anguish, heartaches, or suffering. And when is the best time to rejoice? The present moment is always the appropriate one—it's always the right time to praise our Lord with genuine joy in our hearts, with a prayer of thanksgiving on our lips.

Pray with joy that each of us has the privilege of *participating* in the gospel and not just *hearing* it. Not only do we take in the free gift of grace, but we are also instructed to live out that grace that we have received. Please defend the Good News and rejoice as you share what Jesus has done through you.

Have you made the choice to rejoice? Have you found "the peace that passes all understanding," the genuine assurance that allows you to find pockets of joy during times of suffering? I pray that you have. I pray that you will focus, not on today's troubles, which will inevitably pass, but on God's promise of eternal glory, which has no boundary and no end. And, I pray that you, too, will trust the Lord when He promises that "the sufferings of this present time are not worth comparing with the glory that is to be revealed."

LIGHT FOR OUR PATH FROM GOD'S WORD

For our light and momentary troubles are achieving for us an eternal glory that far outweighs them all.

2 Corinthians 4:17 NIV

I thank my God upon every remembrance of you, always in every prayer of mine making request for you all with joy, for your fellowship in the gospel from the first day until now, being confident of this very thing, that He who has begun a good work in you will complete it until the day of Jesus Christ.

Philippians 1:3-6 NKJV

Not only that, but we rejoice in our sufferings, knowing that suffering produces endurance, and endurance produces character, and character produces hope.

Romans 5:3-4 ESV

Though the fig tree should not blossom and there be no fruit on the vines, though the yield of the olive should fail and the fields produce no food, though the flock should be cut off from the fold and there be no cattle in the stalls, yet I will exult in the Lord, I will rejoice in the God of my salvation.

(Gini cross stitched this verse for us twenty years ago;

God was preparing us for this season!)

Habakkuk 3:17-18 NASB

For this day is holy to our Lord. And do not be grieved, for the joy of the Lord is your strength.

Nehemiah 8:10 ESV

The Lord is my strength and my shield; my heart trusts in Him, and I am helped; therefore my heart exults, and with my song I shall thank Him.

Psalm 28:7 NASB

These things I have spoken to you, that My joy may remain in you, and that your joy may be full.

John 15:11 NKJV

Make a joyful noise unto the LORD, all ye lands. Serve the LORD with gladness: come before his presence with singing.

Psalm 100:1-2 KJV

Is anyone among you suffering? He should pray.

James 5:13 HCSB

Their sorrow was turned into rejoicing and their mourning into a holiday. They were to be days of feasting, rejoicing, and of sending gifts to one another and the poor.

Esther 9:22 HCSB

Rejoice in the Lord always. I will say it again: Rejoice!

Philippians 4:4 HCSB

MORE IMPORTANT IDEAS ABOUT JOY

True joy is not a thing of moods, not a capricious emotion, tied to fluctuating experiences. It is a state and condition of the soul.

Rufus Matthew Jones

Joy is a by-product not of happy circumstances, education or talent, but of a healthy relationship with God and a determination to love Him no matter what.

Barbara Johnson

Jesus did not promise to change the circumstances around us. He promised great peace and pure joy to those who would learn to believe that God actually controls all things.

Corrie ten Boom

Joy is not mere happiness. Nor does joy spring from a life of ease, comfort, or peaceful circumstances. Joy is the soul's buoyant response to a God of promise, presence, and power.

Susan Lenzkes

Finding joy means first of all finding Jesus.

Jill Briscoe

Joy in life is not the absence
of sorrow. The fact that Jesus
could have joy in the midst
of sorrow is proof that we can
experience this too.

—

Warren Wiersbe

GINI'S JOURNEY

May Jesus Be Praised!

Recently, on a rainy Sunday morning, Gini and I got up just as dawn was breaking. The skies cleared, and I began to say the words of a favorite hymn and, as always, I stumbled over the exact words. Gini joined in, remembering the words by heart, along with the melody, too.

> When morning gilds the skies,
> My heart awakening cries,
> May Jesus Christ be praised.

As we stood there, Gini and I felt the Lord's presence, and we felt the prayers of our family and friends.

Some people have asked me how we have been able *not* to worry about the outcome of the various treatments and tests that have resulted from Gini's cancer. As an answer to that question, our youngest daughter, Heather, reminded me of what she sees in us. Heather observed that we can avoid anxiety because we have prepared ourselves *in advance*—with the Lord's help, of course. This has been a pattern of our lives, "resolving" beforehand how to respond to a situation before it arises. Daniel did this in resolving not to eat the king's rich food, and then was able to resist the temptation, ultimately for good. It's important to rest, knowing that the Lord has filled your cup to over-flowing, so that when it is "bumped," it spills out good.

We can cast our cares on the Lord because He cares for us as 1 Peter 5:7 promises. We also purpose to set our minds on things above, resting in His current provision for every need, and we look back on all the promises of God that we have seen Him keep in our lives.

As we waited for the results of Gini's latest test to de-termine if the cancer had returned, a PET Scan, we were at peace. No matter the result, we know it is part of God's perfect plan for our lives on this journey here on earth.

In a recent sermon, based on Ecclesiastes 3:1-15, Brett reminded us that there is a beginning and an ending to all things, including this life. But the ending of this earthly journey is just the beginning of life eternal with the Lord.

The Lord saved us, and we experienced a new begin-ning in the midst of this earthly life. We thank the Lord that He awakened our hearts and that He has put the knowledge of eternity in our hearts.

May Jesus Christ be praised!

CHAPTER 25

—◦—

Thankful for Every Gift

It is good to give thanks to the Lord,
And to sing praises to Your name, O Most High;
To declare Your lovingkindness in the morning,
And Your faithfulness every night.

—

Psalm 92:1-2 NKJV

A LESSON FOR THE JOURNEY

—◦—

The Lord knows what we need, now and forever.
So, every one of God's gifts has a purpose.

Gini's illness has resulted in many examinations and quite a few lengthy tests. Throughout her treatment, we have tried to be faithful servants of the Lord, whether the test results were—from our perspective—positive or negative. Of course, we always rejoiced when test results indicated that her treatments were working as intended. But, even on those heart-wrenching days when treatments had to be stopped because of side effects or test results indicated the tumor was coming back, we still gave thanks (sometimes through our tears). We know that every gift comes from God, in His own timing, for our ultimate good and for His glory—even those gifts that we cannot understand.

Along the way (and especially now that the tumor is coming back), many people have suggested alternative treatments, mostly *natural* based. All treatments (including radiation and chemotherapy drugs) are part of what God has created and allowed, and are therefore *natural*. My perspective is that you cannot chase every rainbow looking for that pot of gold. My children will tell you that I passed on my upbringing that included no sugar cereals and lots of natural and fresh foods, avoiding processed foods, and the like. I lectured on my five principles for good living: No simple sugar, no added salt, no smoking, modified vegetarian diet with emphasis on fish and chicken, and exercise.

We are thankful for *whatever* the Lord allows in our lives because He is in charge and He knows what we need—not what we want, or sometimes *really* do not want! We continue to learn that there is a purpose in all that has happened, is happening, and will happen.

Every gift we receive from the Lord is a bit like a check to be deposited in our account. Just as we would endorse the check, we must respond to divine gifts, taking some action in order to use the gift the Lord has provided. We cannot just leave God's gift in a corner untouched. We believe that we have been blessed so that we might, in some way, be a blessing to others.

After her surgery, when Gini and I received good news that her cancer was nearly entirely removed; and after she had passed several medical milestones with no tumor reappearing, we both realized that, with this gift, she and I must focus on living because it had become apparent that the Lord was not yet ready to carry her home. So, Gini decided to continue to serve God to the best of her abilities, however He allows, for the rest of her life. We all need to take this attitude and live out the life the Lord has given to us. Although our gifts may change, we all need to utilize our gifts, even when we would sometimes prefer to give up on life.

Gini and I have studied and taught James and 1 Peter several times. These two books, along with many other passages in the Bible, teach us that the Lord is our Treasure, a sacred Gift that must not be hoarded, hidden, or kept for ourselves. Instead, we must use this special gift of Christ within us. So, we don't study the Bible to gain knowledge, alone. We study God's Word to apply His truth to our lives as we live for Him and His purposes, not our own.

I am thankful for one example given to me many years ago. We are to be "water pipes" of the Lord with His "Living Water" flowing through us. Simple enough, but there are two problems we continually face: inflow and outflow. Regarding inflow, we must remember to constantly seek the Lord by study of His Word, and then asking Him to show us how to apply His truth so there is no slowing or shutting off of the Source. Regarding outflow, we need to serve "water" rather than storing it; we need to be ready to share. Otherwise, we are like the Dead Sea, having only inflow, but no outflow.

Please do not shut off your own faucet; instead, make sure that you share the "water" you have been given so that even more can flow through you.

LIGHT FOR OUR PATH FROM GOD'S WORD

Therefore as you have received Christ Jesus the Lord, walk in Him, rooted and built up in Him and established in the faith, just as you were taught, and overflowing with thankfulness.

Colossians 2:6-7 HCSB

Jesus answered her, "If you knew the gift of God, and who it is that is saying to you, 'Give me a drink,' you would have asked him, and he would have given you living water."

John 4:10 ESV

If anyone is thirsty, he should come to Me and drink! The one who believes in Me, as the Scripture has said, will have streams of living water flow from deep within him.

John 7:37-38 HCSB

Now may the God of hope fill you with all joy and peace as you believe in Him so that you may overflow with hope by the power of the Holy Spirit.

Romans 15:13 HCSB

Let the peace of Christ rule in your hearts, since as members of one body you were called to peace. And be thankful.

Colossians 3:15 NIV

In everything give thanks; for this is the will of God in Christ Jesus for you.

1 Thessalonians 5:18 NKJV

Through Him then, let us continually offer up a sacrifice of praise to God, that is, the fruit of lips that give thanks to His name.

Hebrews 13:15 NASB

For the Lord God is a sun and shield. The Lord gives grace and glory; He does not withhold the good from those who live with integrity. Lord of Hosts, happy is the person who trusts in You!

Psalm 84:11-12 HCSB

Every good gift and every perfect gift is from above, coming down from the Father of lights.

James 1:17 ESV

Love the Lord your God with all your heart, with all your soul, and with all your strength. These words that I am giving you today are to be in your heart. Repeat them to your children. Talk about them when you sit in your house and when you walk along the road, when you lie down and when you get up.

Deuteronomy 6:5-7 HCSB

MORE IMPORTANT IDEAS ABOUT
BEING THANKFUL

The heathen misrepresent God by worshipping idols; we misrepresent God by our murmuring and our complaining.

C. H. Spurgeon

Active faith gives thanks for a promise even though it is not yet performed, knowing that God's contracts are as good as cash.

Matthew Henry

The words "thank" and "think" come from the same root word. If we would think more, we would thank more.

Warren Wiersbe

The unthankful heart discovers no mercies; but the thankful heart will find, in every hour, some heavenly blessings!

Henry Ward Beecher

A Christian who walks by faith accepts all circumstances from God. He thanks God when everything goes good, when everything goes bad, and for the "blues" somewhere in between. He thanks God whether he feels like it or not.

Erwin Lutzer

When it comes to life,
the critical thing is whether you
take things for granted or
take them with gratitude.

———

G. K. Chesterton

GINI'S JOURNEY

The Gift of Teaching

In 1 Peter 4:10-11, we are told, "Each of you has been blessed with one or more of God's many wonderful gifts, to be used in the service of others. So use your gift well. If you have the gift of speaking, preach God's message. If you have the gift of helping others, do it with the strength that God supplies. Everything should be done in a way that will bring honor to God because of Jesus Christ, who is glorious and powerful forever. Amen" (ESV).

We each receive different gifts, and those gifts may vary during our lifetimes. But, one thing doesn't change: when we receive a gift from the Lord, we have a responsibility to use that gift properly.

One of Gini's gifts is her talent for teaching. When our girls were teenagers, she and I held Bible studies together with our daughters and with other teenagers. Later, we both participated in, wrote, and taught, inductive Bible studies for adults; teaching in our home here in Anderson and in the home of Marcia and Dave in Australia.

Gini also taught Sunday school 25 years, mostly to second- and third-graders. Many of her students give testimony of her faithfulness in teaching God's Word to them and her emphasis on memorization and Bible study.

Today, Gini still has the gift of teaching, but it has a different "face" or appearance. Now, she is teaching us how to live faithfully and peacefully amid the storms of life. Despite her illness, despite her limitations in processing and connecting, despite the various discomforts she endures each day, Gini is now teaching us how to smile, how to pray, how to praise, and how to live. Her countenance and peace are obvious as she walks with her Lord through the valley of the shadow of death. Her twinkling eyes and her beautiful smile teach volumes.

And whatever you do, in word or in deed,
do everything in the name of the Lord Jesus,
giving thanks to God the Father through Him.

—

Colossians 3:17 HCSB

CHAPTER 26

Praise Him

Enter into His gates with thanksgiving,
and into His courts with praise. Be thankful to Him,
and bless His name. For the Lord is good;
His mercy is everlasting, and His truth endures
to all generations.

—

Psalm 100:4-5 NKJV

A LESSON FOR THE JOURNEY

We have the privilege of praising a faithful,
wise, good, and loving God
in every circumstance.

P salm 147:1 proclaims, "Praise the Lord! For it is good to sing praises to our God; for it is pleasant, and a song of praise is fitting" (ESV).

Since the Lord called us to Himself, I can truthfully say that Gini and I have praised the Lord in the midst of *all* our circumstances. We have experienced moments of despair, fear, and disappointments (who hasn't?), but from the first day we found out about her brain tumor until now, we both have rested in the Lord, seeing Him as both the Giver and Protector of life. Decisions to stop or reduce treatments have been difficult, but each time the Lord has allowed for side effects or hazards that prevented those treatments or the amounts of treatment. And, we have trusted that He will carry us home from this earthly journey at a time of His choosing. We have many reasons to praise Him in every season of life.

We know that every day the Lord is guiding and providing for us. During the happiest times, we give praise for His blessings. And during the very difficult days, we give praise for His promise of eternal life. For we know that our journey through this world is but a brief instant when compared to eternity.

We also praise God for the constant support of family and friends. We are genuinely thankful for all of their prayers, their visits, their notes, and their e-mails. We are thankful that the Lord has seen fit to support us in this way.

We have found it easy to praise the Lord because we trust Him. We know that He loves us. We know, without any doubt, that there is a reason for everything. We have a Sovereign God, in charge of absolutely every detail, and we know that His way is the perfect way.

Psalm 33:1 instructs us to, "Shout for joy in the Lord, O you righteous! Praise befits the upright" (ESV). Gini and I find countless reasons to praise God every day, and I pray that you will see many reasons to praise Him, too. I pray that today you will lift your prayers to Him and thank Him for who He is and for all that He has done. Praise Him in good times and tough times because His plan is perfect, His blessings are beyond understanding, and His love endures forever.

LIGHT FOR OUR PATH FROM GOD'S WORD

Praise the Lord, all nations! Extol him, all peoples! For great is his steadfast love toward us, and the faithfulness of the Lord endures forever. Praise the Lord!

Psalm 117 ESV

Sing praises to God, sing praises: sing praises unto our King, sing praises. For God is the King of all the earth: sing ye praises with understanding.

Psalm 47:6-7 KJV

Therefore, whether we are at home or away, we make it our aim to be pleasing to Him.

2 Corinthians 5:9 HCSB

Praise the Lord. Give thanks to the Lord, for he is good; his love endures forever.

Psalm 106:1 NIV

But as for me, I will always have hope; I will praise you more and more.

Psalm 71:14 NIV

Give thanks in all circumstances; for this is God's will for you in Christ Jesus.

1 Thessalonians 5:18 NIV

*Through Him then, let us continually
offer up a sacrifice of praise to God,
that is, the fruit of lips
that give thanks to His name.*

—

Hebrews 13:15 NASB

MORE IMPORTANT IDEAS ABOUT PRAISE

Praise—lifting up our heart and hands, exulting with our voices, singing his praises—is the occupation of those who dwell in the kingdom.

Max Lucado

A child of God should be a visible beatitude for joy and a living doxology for gratitude.

C. H. Spurgeon

Praise is not only speaking to the Lord on our own account, but it is praising Him for what He has done for others.

D. L. Moody

Our God is the sovereign Creator of the universe! He loves us as His own children and has provided every good thing we have; He is worthy of our praise every moment.

Shirley Dobson

Holy, holy, holy! Lord God Almighty! All Thy works shall praise Thy name in earth, and sky, and sea.

Reginald Heber

On earth join all ye creatures to extol Him first, Him last, Him midst, and without end.

John Milton

GINI'S JOURNEY

Thankful for the Years

In December 2012, Gini and I began our fiftieth year of married life together. She and I continue to praise the Lord, not only for the gift of time together on this earth, but also for the priceless gift of time together with our Lord, forever, in heaven.

We are viewing this year as our Biblical equivalent of "The Year of Jubilee." Leviticus 25:10 says, "This fiftieth year is sacred—it is a time of freedom and of celebration when everyone will receive back their original property, and slaves will return home to their families" (CEV).

Our goal is to celebrate our fiftieth all year long, even as we embrace the physical suffering and emotional pain of the return of the tumor. Should weakness and confusion return with the regrowth of Gini's tumor, we will face the hard decision: when to remove, reduce, or when to stop treatment. The Lord gave us the privilege of using treatments, and He also gives us the privilege of stopping, but the second decision is always hard for any of us to make. It will be especially hard because of our years together; we have come to love each other so much! However God chooses to bless us, whatever way He chooses to purify us, we will give thanks and praise Him. The Lord is preparing us for heaven as He leads us on our earthly journey, wherever that journey may take us.

In the past, there were times when we put our confidence in the things of this world, and we were always disappointed. When we took our own path of self-reliance, thinking that we had control over our "happiness," it led to pain and dissatisfaction. As objects of His mercy, we praise God that He revealed to us a far better way: *His* way.

Now we know that true joy and thankfulness are not created by our own efforts or because of our own accomplishments. Worldly things, whether material riches or physical health, are fading more and more each day. Our true riches result from a personal relationship with our Lord, a relationship that is built on the sure foundation and rock-solid strength of Jesus Christ. We praise Him for continuing to work through and bless us as we go through cancer, chemo, relapse . . .

CHAPTER 27

The Direction of Your Thoughts

*And the peace of God, which surpasses every thought,
will guard your hearts and your minds in Christ Jesus.
Finally brothers, whatever is true, whatever is honorable,
whatever is just, whatever is pure, whatever is lovely,
whatever is commendable—if there is any moral excellence
and if there is any praise—dwell on these things.*

—

Philippians 4:7-8 HCSB

A LESSON FOR THE JOURNEY

The quality and direction of your thoughts
will determine, to a satisfying extent,
the quality and direction of your life.

The Bible teaches that we can, and should, take control of our thoughts by "taking them captive." In the tenth chapter of 2 Corinthians, we are told, "For the weapons of our warfare are not of the flesh but have divine power to destroy strongholds. We destroy arguments and every lofty opinion raised against the knowledge of God, *and take every thought captive* to obey Christ" (emphasis mine, vv. 4-5 ESV).

It is easier to talk about controlling our thoughts than it is to actually control them, especially during times of suffering. After all, it can be hard to give thanks for the things that we, with our limited understanding, wish had not happened. And, it can be hard not to worry about the things that we fear. Hard, but not impossible.

Thankfully, God's Word has specific instructions which can help us redirect destructive thoughts before they can do us harm. God starts by telling us to lift up the "shield of faith" in every season of life: "In all circumstances take up the shield of faith, with which you can extinguish all the flaming darts of the evil one; and take the helmet of salvation, and the sword of the Spirit, which is the word of God, praying at all times in the Spirit, with all prayer and supplication" (Ephesians 6:16-18 ESV).

The Bible also instructs us to focus our thoughts on things that are honorable, pure, lovely, and commendable, as is directed in Philippians 4 (see above). In other words,

God wants us to count our blessings, not to take inventory of and dwell on our troubles.

Furthermore, the Bible teaches us to rely on hope: "Blessed be the God and Father of our Lord Jesus Christ! According to his great mercy, he has caused us to be born again to a living hope through the resurrection of Jesus Christ from the dead, to an inheritance that is imperishable, undefiled, and unfading, kept in heaven for you, who by God's power are being guarded through faith for a salvation ready to be revealed in the last time" (1 Peter 1:3-5 ESV).

John Piper has written a book that I heartily recommend. It's called *Think*. In it, Piper asks each reader to examine his or her life's purpose in light of the following verses from the second chapter of Philippians. These verses teach us to have the mind of Christ and to sense (see, hear, taste, and feel) His truth as we apply it to the way we think and act:

So if there is any encouragement in Christ, any comfort from love, any participation in the Spirit, any affection and sympathy, complete my joy by being of the same mind, having the same love, being in full accord and of one mind. Do nothing from selfish ambition or conceit, but in humility count others more significant than yourselves. Let each of you look not only to his own interests, but also to the interests of others. Have this mind among yourselves, which is yours in Christ Jesus, who, though he was in the form of God, did not count equality with God a thing to be grasped, but emptied himself, by taking the form of a servant, being born in the likeness of men. And being found in human form, he humbled himself by becoming obedient to the point of death, even death on a cross. Therefore God has highly exalted him and bestowed on him the name that is above every name, so that at the name of Jesus every knee should bow, in heaven and on earth and under the earth, and every tongue confess that Jesus Christ is Lord, to the glory of God the Father. Therefore, my beloved, as you have always obeyed, so now, not only as in my presence but much more in my absence, work out your own salvation with fear and trembling, for it is God who works in you, both to will and to work for his good pleasure. Do all things without grumbling or disputing, that you may be blameless and innocent, children of God without blemish in the midst of a crooked and twisted generation, among whom you shine as lights in the world, holding fast to the word of life, so that in the day of Christ I may be proud that I did not run in vain or labor in vain. (vv. 1-11 ESV)

This passage reminds you to "do all things without grumbling or disputing." And, it asks you to allow the Lord to direct your thoughts. It's God's design; it is the best way to live, *and* it's the proper way to think.

I beseech you therefore, brethren, by the mercies of God, that you present your bodies a living sacrifice, holy, acceptable to God, which is your reasonable service. And do not be conformed to this world, but be transformed by the renewing of your mind, that you may prove what is that good and acceptable and perfect will of God.

—

Romans 12:1-2 NKJV

LIGHT FOR OUR PATH FROM GOD'S WORD

We destroy arguments and every lofty opinion raised against the knowledge of God, and take every thought captive to obey Christ.

2 Corinthians 2:5 ESV

Jesus replied, "'Love the Lord your God with all your heart and with all your soul and with all your mind.' This is the first and greatest commandment. And the second is like it: 'Love your neighbor as yourself.' All the Law and the Prophets hang on these two commandments."

Matthew 22:37-40 NIV

Commit your works to the Lord, and your thoughts will be established.

Proverbs 16:3 NKJV

Why am I so depressed? Why this turmoil within me? Put your hope in God, for I will still praise Him, my Savior and my God.

Psalm 42:11 HCSB

In thee, O Lord, do I put my trust; let me never be put into confusion.

Psalm 71:1 KJV

MORE IMPORTANT IDEAS ABOUT
THE DIRECTION OF YOUR THOUGHTS

Sow a thought and you reap an action; sow an act and you reap a habit; sow a habit and you reap a character; sow a character and you reap a destiny.

Ralph Waldo Emerson

Every major spiritual battle is in the mind.

Charles Stanley

The majority of us recognize the necessity of receiving the Holy Spirit for living, but we do not sufficiently recognize the need for drawing on the resources of the Holy Spirit for thinking.

Oswald Chambers

I became aware of one very important concept I had missed before: my attitude—not my circumstances—was what was making me unhappy.

Vonette Bright

No more imperfect thoughts. No more sad memories. No more ignorance. My redeemed body will have a redeemed mind. Grant me a foretaste of that perfect mind as you mirror your thoughts in me today.

Joni Eareckson Tada

It is the thoughts
and intents of the heart
that shape a person's life.

—

John Eldredge

GINI'S JOURNEY

Still Smiling

Gini has continued to smile throughout her hardship. Even when her thoughts have been confused, her faith and dignity have shown through to family, to friends, and to strangers.

After the recurrence of Gini's tumor, our daughter Kim said this clearly in an e-mail:

My mom continues to live well in spite of the brain tumor that was discovered nearly two years ago. Last week, an MRI showed that, after a blessed break from treatments, the tumor is growing back. There have been, and will be, many decisions to make. She has been gracious and sweet through all this. All women should be loved and cared for as she is by my dad. He's writing a book about their experience with trials, and it's changing him for the better as he continues to run to God throughout such a hard time.

Kim's description of Gini is accurate: my wife has been "gracious and sweet" through this ordeal. Her journey has been incredibly difficult, but Gini's faith has not been shaken.

I'd like to repeat (from a different translation) the scripture passage that began this chapter because it's a verse Gini has memorized: "Finally, brothers, whatever is true, whatever is honorable, whatever is just, whatever is pure, whatever is lovely, whatever is commendable, if there is any excellence, if there is anything worthy of praise, *think* about these things. What you have learned and received and heard and seen in me—*practice* these things, and the God of peace will be with you" (Philippians 4:8-9, ESV, emphasis mine).

Because Gini is thinking these thoughts, God is using her so that you might continue to see, hear, learn, and receive His truth through her. She can keep smiling that beautiful smile through the most difficult days, knowing that God is good and that He will protect her now and forever. She would ask that you *think* God's thoughts, and preach His Word to your heart. When falsehood and the noise of life enter in, you will clearly hear and know the beat of your Father's heart.

CHAPTER 28

✑

He Is Here

*Have I not commanded you? Be strong and
of good courage; do not be afraid, nor be dismayed,
for the Lord your God is with you wherever you go.*

—

Joshua 1:9 NKJV

A LESSON FOR THE JOURNEY

✑

On your journey home, God never leaves
your side, not even for an instant. He is with you
always, now, and throughout eternity.

The first words from Psalm 46 are so familiar, but I never grow tired of hearing them: "God is our refuge and strength, a very present help in trouble" (ESV). It's comforting to know that God is "very present," that He's always not just near, but here, beside us wherever we are. He is our strength and our shield against suffering.

Later in Psalm 46, the Lord instructs us to, "Be still and know that I am God." During those quiet moments, we begin to sense the loving presence of our Creator, and we are reassured by the certain knowledge that God is who He says He is, and that He is, quite literally, here.

Oswald Chambers observed, "The spiritual life is not a measurable product, but a dynamic process." Indeed, we need to make our faith dynamic by seeking, walking, praying, rejoicing, giving thanks, and sensing the Lord's presence in every aspect of our lives. And wherever our journey takes us, God is an all-surrounding Presence, holding our hand.

God's ever-present help is made clear in the beautiful words of Psalm 23:4: "Yea, though I walk through the valley of the shadow of death, I will fear no evil: for thou art with me; thy rod and thy staff they comfort me" (KJV). God does not exempt us from the valleys of life, but neither does He ask us to walk alone. He is always there!

As Gini and I travel hand-in-hand past continuing milestones, we know that God, through His Spirit, is with us always. And, we know that the end of our earthly journey is not really "the end." We can rejoice in every circumstance because we know that the Lord cares for us from birth to death and beyond! What a joy it is to trust these promises. What a blessing to know that He is here.

For I am persuaded that neither death nor life,
nor angels nor rulers, nor things present,
nor things to come, nor powers, nor height,
nor depth, nor any other created thing will have
the power to separate us from the love of God
that is in Christ Jesus our Lord!

—

Romans 8:38-39 HCSB

LIGHT FOR OUR PATH FROM GOD'S WORD

The eyes of the Lord are in every place, keeping watch . . . .

Proverbs 15:3 NKJV

Fear not, for I am with you; Be not dismayed, for I am your God. I will strengthen you.

Isaiah 41:10 NKJV

The Lord is with you when you are with Him. If you seek Him, He will be found by you.

2 Chronicles 15:2 HCSB

For where two or three are gathered together in my name, there am I in the midst of them.

Matthew 18:20 KJV

I am not alone, because the Father is with me.

John 16:32 KJV

The LORD's unfailing love surrounds the man who trusts in him.

Psalm 32:10 NIV

God is faithful, by whom you were called into the fellowship of His Son Jesus Christ our Lord.

1 Corinthians 1:9 NKJV

MORE IMPORTANT IDEAS ABOUT
GOD'S PRESENCE

You need not cry very loud; He is nearer to us than we think.

Brother Lawrence

God is at work; He is in full control; He is in the midst of whatever has happened, is happening, and will happen.

Charles Swindoll

The Lord Jesus by His Holy Spirit is with me, and the knowledge of His presence dispels the darkness and allays any fears.

Bill Bright

There is nothing more important in any life than the constantly enjoyed presence of the Lord. There is nothing more vital, for without it we shall make mistakes, and without it we shall be defeated.

Alan Redpath

I have a capacity in my soul for taking in God entirely. I am as sure as I live that nothing is so near to me as God. God is nearer to me than I am to myself; my existence depends on the nearness and the presence of God.

Meister Eckhart

We need never shout across
the spaces to an absent God.
He is nearer than our own soul,
closer than our most
secret thoughts.

—

A. W. Tozer

GINI'S JOURNEY

He Is With Us

Recently, while holding Gini's hand, I reminded her that we are on the way to our destination. And as we journey together, the Lord is holding our hands as well (and a cord of three strands is not easily broken—we are thankful for the tie that binds us together through Christ Jesus).

There will come a time for both of us to complete our journey on our own, but when that time comes, even then the Lord will be holding our hand as we walk through that valley past the final milestone of this worldly journey.

Jesus is reaching out to you. Our prayer is that, even now, you will see He is holding your hand as you pass every milestone on your own journey home.

The following page contains the lyrics from one of Gini's favorite hymns. These words remind us that Christ is sufficient to meet all our needs, and that His love has no limits.

HE GIVETH MORE GRACE
By Annie Flynt

He giveth more grace as our burdens grow greater,
He sendeth more strength as our labors increase;
To added afflictions He addeth His mercy,
To multiplied trials He multiplies peace.

When we have exhausted our store of endurance,
When our strength has failed ere the day is half done,
When we reach the end of our hoarded resources
Our Father's full giving is only begun.

Fear not that thy need shall exceed His provision,
Our God ever yearns His resources to share;
Lean hard on the arm everlasting, availing;
The Father both thee and thy load will upbear.

His love has no limits, His grace has no measure,
His power no boundary known unto men;
For out of His infinite riches in Jesus
He giveth, and giveth, and giveth again.

CHAPTER 29

—◦—

This Is the Day

This is the day the L<small>ORD</small> has made;
we will rejoice and be glad in it.

—

Psalm 118:24 NKJV

A LESSON FOR THE JOURNEY

—◦—

Every day is a gift from God,
a gift that should be enjoyed and celebrated.

I have told you about when Gini was first diagnosed with cancer, and about discovering the cancer has returned, and about treatments we can no longer use. It was difficult to proclaim that the Lord had, indeed, made those days—and to rejoice and be glad in each of those days. But, He indeed has made each day!

Gini and I made the decision to trust the Lord and to follow Him as we continue our journey through our remaining days together on this earth. Despite the circumstances—and even during those moments when we were overcome with sadness—we both agreed to treat each remaining day as a precious gift from God. So now, we are enjoying each day that the Lord is giving us. And, we are celebrating the opportunity to communicate with family, with friends, and with you.

When asked if we are sometimes sad, we answer that, indeed, we are. As we continue to walk through our life-journey together and with the Lord, we are both in some stage of grieving, and even writing this book (to which Gini has been able to make contributions along the way) has helped. But, in relation to 1 Thessalonians 4:13, Gini said, "I do not grieve as one without hope. My hope is faith based on nothing less than Jesus; that faith is rest and trust in what God will provide."

Our journey home is a bit like taking a long hike. We take along a guidebook and other aids, and we make plans for provision and protection. As we walk, the path is sometimes sunny, smooth, and pleasant, yet sometimes stormy, steep, and difficult. We know that wherever we find ourselves, the Lord is there with us. We strive to stay on the path He has chosen for us, and we are determined to walk with Him over every hill and through every valley. Every day, we encounter other travelers, some walking alongside, others passing in the opposite direction. Whenever we are given a God-appointed opportunity, we share what we've learned and try to help fellow travelers find sure footing as we encourage them to press on—or change to our direction and join us.

Because we know we are forever blessed, we can celebrate every stage of the journey, certain that nothing can separate us from our Father's love. We rejoice during these great days the Lord has provided us, and we thank Him for allowing us to be part of His army on this earth.

The 118th Psalm reminds us that today, like every other day, is a cause for celebration. God gives us this day; He fills it to the brim with possibilities, and He invites us to use it for His purposes. Each day is like the talents parable. The Lord asks us to properly invest every minute, taking advantage of every opportunity. Once the day is gone, it's gone forever. Our responsibility is to use our time wisely, in service of the Lord, as we journey toward home.

My prayer for you today is that you will treasure the

time that God has given you and your loved ones. Praise God and remember the pleasant days. Cherish each moment, even when the valley is dark or the path is rocky. Give God the glory and thank Him for what He has done. And, search for the hidden possibilities that the Lord has placed along your path. Remember that today is a priceless gift from the Father; rejoice as you walk and encourage others: *This is the day the Lord has made . . . .*

So, whether you eat or drink, or whatever you do, do all to the glory of God.

—

1 Corinthians 10:31 ESV

LIGHT FOR OUR PATH FROM GOD'S WORD

Thou wilt show me the path of life: in thy presence is fulness of joy; at thy right hand there are pleasures for evermore.

Psalm 16:11 KJV

So teach us to number our days, that we may gain a heart of wisdom.

Psalm 90:12 NKJV

I have come that they may have life, and that they may have it more abundantly.

John 10:10 NKJV

And God is able to make all grace abound to you, so that always having all sufficiency in everything, you may have an abundance for every good deed.

2 Corinthians 9:8 NASB

But as it is written: "Eye has not seen, nor ear heard, nor have entered into the heart of man the things which God has prepared for those who love Him."

1 Corinthians 2:9 NKJV

But now I come to You, and these things I speak in the world, that they may have My joy fulfilled in themselves.

John 17:13 NKJV

MORE IMPORTANT IDEAS ABOUT
CELEBRATING TODAY

It is not hard for the Lord to turn night into day. He that sends the clouds can as easily clear the skies. Let us be encouraged. Things are better down the road. Let us sing praises to our God in anticipation . . .

Charles Spurgeon

Jesus intended for us to be overwhelmed by the blessings of regular days. He said it was the reason he had come: "I am come that they might have life, and that they might have it more abundantly."

Gloria Gaither

Every day should be a fantastic adventure for us because we're in the middle of God's unfolding plan for the ages.

John MacArthur

May this day be for me a day of obedience and of charity, a day of happiness and peace. May all my walk and conversation be such as becometh the gospel of Christ.

John Baillie

Every day we live is a priceless gift of God, loaded with possibilities to learn something new, to gain fresh insights.

Dale Evans Rogers

GINI'S JOURNEY

Walk with Joy

Gini and I find it easy to celebrate life here on earth because we often remind ourselves of the life that is yet to be: eternal life in heaven.

In Peter's second letter, it is apparent that the author is fully cognizant, not only of his own death, but also of his everlasting life in Christ. In fact, the entire epistle serves as instruction about the end of our life on this earth, and what we are to be doing for the Lord *before* putting off this earthly body. We are praying you, too, might seek the Lord this very day while recalling His truth, love, kindness *and* His very great promises.

Peter's words are both instructional and comforting to Gini and me because they serve as a reminder of the things the Lord has done and continues to do through the life we have shared. We walk with joy, peace, and hope, holding hands and meeting fellow travelers. We are sharing the Lord and seeing Him lead, direct, provide, and strengthen us on our journey home.

His divine power has granted to us all things that pertain to life and godliness, through the knowledge of him who called us to his own glory and excellence, by which he has granted to us his precious and very great promises, so that through them you may become partakers of the divine nature, having escaped from the corruption that is in the world because of sinful desire. For this very reason, make every effort to supplement your faith with virtue, and virtue with knowledge, and knowledge with self-control, and self-control with steadfastness, and steadfastness with godliness, and godliness with brotherly affection, and brotherly affection with love. For if these qualities are yours and are increasing, they keep you from being ineffective or unfruitful in the knowledge of our Lord Jesus Christ.

For whoever lacks these qualities is so nearsighted that he is blind, having forgotten that he was cleansed from his former sins. Therefore, brothers, be all the more diligent to confirm your calling and election, for if you practice these qualities you will never fall. For in this way there will be richly provided for you an entrance into the eternal kingdom of our Lord and Savior Jesus Christ.

Therefore I intend always to remind you of these qualities, though you know them and are established in the truth that you have. I think it right, as long as I am in this body, to stir you up by way of reminder, since I know that the putting off of my body will be soon, as our Lord Jesus Christ made clear to me. And I will make every effort so that after my departure you may be able at any time to recall these things.

2 Peter 1:3-15 ESV

CHAPTER 30

—❧—

Not the Last Chapter

Our citizenship is in heaven,
from which we also eagerly wait for a Savior,
the Lord Jesus Christ.

—

Philippians 3:20 HCSB

A LESSON FOR THE JOURNEY

—❧—

You are on a glorious journey—ordained and orchestrated by God—toward your true home. If you have chosen to follow Jesus, your true home is heaven, and this earthly chapter of your life is not the last.

Gini and I know that we have just begun our journey! We human beings are born; we live for a time, and then we die. Then, we will spend eternity somewhere. Some people believe that death is inevitably "the final chapter" of life, but they are mistaken. The Lord offers eternal life to each of us through His Son.

When CB radio was the craze, I had the "handle" of *Pathfinder*. I was searching for my own path. The Lord helped both Gini and me *find* the right path and guide our every step, past every milestone, through this life on earth.

For many years, Gini and I *thought* we were Christians, but on a mission trip in the 1970s, the Lord changed our lives forever. Now we no longer *think* we are Christians; we *know* we are children of our heavenly King, and we *know* that we will spend eternity with Him. So we can rejoice, even when we are suffering, because of our certainty that this chapter of our lives is not the final one. Cancer can kill the body, and many times it does. But it cannot kill the soul.

Gini and I know our names are in the Lamb's book of life, placed there for all eternity. God has called us to Himself, and we are praying that you might see He is calling you, too.

The Lord offers you Christ and eternal life: a gift that cost so much yet is freely given. No matter where you are, if you are hearing God calling you, my prayer for you today is that you consider your need of Him and see Him transform your life, not only now, but forever.

At the time of this writing, Gini's cancer has returned, but each day is a true blessing. I have retired from my medical practice so I can care for her full-time. For us, many days we do suffer and feel weak, but the joy of the Lord continues to be our strength. And I pray that you will know the Lord and have the peace that passes all understanding, the contentment that comes when you know, right down to the deepest corner of your mind and heart, that this chapter of *your* life is not the last.

Throughout this book, I have written about our family's difficult days with one overriding goal in mind: to help you see Christ, and Christ alone, as your all-sufficient Lord and Savior, the "I AM" who is able to meet every need and answer every question. I have tried to help you see that, because each milestone on your journey has a purpose, it also contains a blessing. And, I have tried to encourage you to treasure each day and to give thanks in every circumstance, while resting and trusting in the Lord.

Although you will inevitably encounter times of suffering and overwhelming trials in this world, you'll celebrate the ultimate victory in eternity. The person and presence of God is our greatest good and the final destination of this earthly journey.

LIGHT FOR OUR PATH FROM GOD'S WORD

In My Father's house are many dwelling places; if not, I would have told you. I am going away to prepare a place for you. If I go away and prepare a place for you, I will come back and receive you to Myself, so that where I am you may be also.

John 14:2-3 HCSB

Your kingdom is an everlasting kingdom, and Your dominion endures throughout all generations.

Psalm 145:13 NASB

Again, the kingdom of heaven is like a merchant in search of fine pearls. When he found one priceless pearl, he went and sold everything he had, and bought it.

Matthew 13:45-46 HCSB

A little while, and ye shall not see me: and again, a little while, and ye shall see me, because I go to the Father.

John 16:16 KJV

He will wipe away every tear from their eyes, and death shall be no more, neither shall there be mourning, nor crying, nor pain anymore, for the former things have passed away.

Revelation 21:4 ESV

The LORD is my shepherd; I shall not want.
He maketh me to lie down in green pastures:
He leadeth me beside the still waters.
He restoreth my soul: He leadeth me in the paths
of righteousness for His name's sake.
Yea, though I walk through the valley of the shadow
of death, I will fear no evil: for Thou art with me;
Thy rod and Thy staff they comfort me.
Thou preparest a table before me in the presence
of mine enemies: Thou anointest my head with oil;
my cup runneth over. Surely goodness and mercy
shall follow me all the days of my life:
and I will dwell in the house of the LORD forever.

—

23rd Psalm

MORE IMPORTANT IDEAS ABOUT
THE PROMISE OF HEAVEN

Even life's happiest experiences last but a moment, yet Heaven's joy is eternal. Some day we will go to our eternal Home, and Christ will be there to welcome us!

Billy Graham

My story. Your story. How it is told in the end and what the story says depends on what each of us does with Jesus.

Gloria Gaither

Considering how I prepare for my children when I know they are coming home, I love to think of the preparations God is making for my homecoming one day.

Anne Graham Lotz

Heaven itself will reflect the character of our great God. It will be a place of holiness, righteousness, love, justice, mercy, peace, order, and His sovereign rule.

Bill Bright

The believing Christian has hope as he stands at the grave of a loved one who is with the Lord, for he knows that the separation is not forever. It is a glorious truth that those who are in Christ never see each other for the last time.

Billy Graham

What joy that the Bible tells us
the great comfort that
the best is yet to be.
Our outlook goes
beyond this world.

———

Corrie ten Boom

GINI'S JOURNEY

Rest and Trust

Recently, I again asked Gini what advice she had for readers of this book, fellow travelers. It was the same counsel she had given when I first asked her what she was thinking as we started this trial. And, it was the same wisdom she has shared with countless friends. She said, "Trust and rest in the Lord in all things. Study God's Word, and put scripture in your heart, because you will need it for the journey."

These words touched me deeply because I realized that, for many years, Gini had already been taking her own advice. For years, she had trusted the Lord completely, studied His Word continuously, and memorized hundreds of verses. So, when cancer struck, she was prepared. In fact, she was again teaching a Bible study group based on a book, *Trusting God* by Jerry Bridges.

Gini's smile continues to warm the hearts of family and friends. And the testimony of her life in Christ continues to be a blessing to everybody she encounters.

God has been so good to Gini and me, and we remain profoundly grateful because we know that God has prepared a place for us. Of course we love our family and friends, and we're not anxious to leave them. But we are excited about the next chapter: We can't wait to see what our heavenly home looks like!

Recently, in a moment of amazing clarity, Gini said, "I cannot save my own life, physical or spiritual. I rest and trust in Jesus, in whom I live and move and have my being."

For me, these words are a fitting testimony to her life, and a fitting conclusion to this text.

May God bless *your* journey home, now and eternally, Amen.

Gene and sister Mary

Gini and brother Virg

1963 Holding Hands

2012 Still Holding Hands
Gene and Gini begin 50th year together

2013 50 Years of Holding Hands!
Campbell, Rod, Chandler, Heather, McCray, Gene, Gini, Elizabeth,
Stephen, Becky, Jim, Ben, Kim, Baillie, Brian, Sam

Foster Sons: Nathan, Wesley, Brian, Travis, siblings and children

About the Author

Dr. Gene Baillie grew up in rural Nebraska, the oldest of six children and the first member of his family to attend college. He and Gini were married during his first year of medical school. After completing medical school, pathology training, and two years of public health service, Gene practiced pathology for 35 years in Anderson, South Carolina. For many years, he taught technologist and pathology courses at a national level, and he was elected to the board of the American Society for Clinical Pathology, serving as their president in 2002-03. He has written several medical articles, including one with his daughter Becky about biblical leprosy.

Gene and Gini raised three biological children, Becky, Kim, and Heather, who are now married have blessed their parents with eight grandchildren. The Baillies also raised four foster sons who were part of a family of eight children. All eight children are considered part of the Baillie family, as are *their* children. The Baillie family also includes many spiritual children and grandchildren as well.

Gene and Gini have been blessed to have traveled on mission trips to Korea, Taiwan, Japan, Jamaica, the Republic of Congo, and Liberia. They have also been a part of planting four churches, including one in Australia, where

Gene worked for five years teaching pathology to medical doctors. He is an elder in the Presbyterian Church in America.

Over the years, the Baillie home has served as a site for newly-started churches and as a place for Gene and Gini to teach inductive Bible studies. For over a quarter of a century, Gene has been passionate about reading the Bible through each year, and he has encouraged many others, by weekly accountability, to do the same.

If you desire to contact the author, please email:
GiniJourneyHome@gmail.com

To order additional copies of this book or
obtain in e-book format, go to:
www.readTheJourneyHome.com